THE SOUL OF
MODERN POETRY

BY

R. H. STRACHAN, D.D.

KENNIKAT PRESS
Port Washington, N. Y./London

THE SOUL OF MODERN POETRY

First published in 1922
Reissued in 1970 by Kennikat Press
Library of Congress Catalog Card No: 70-113348
ISBN 0-8046-1054-1

Manufactured by Taylor Publishing Company   Dallas, Texas

Preface

THE book is founded upon lectures on Twentieth-Century Poets and Poetry, delivered to a general audience in Edinburgh. In the interpretation of George Meredith's poetry, I am deeply indebted to *The Poetry and Philosophy of George Meredith* by G. M. Trevelyan. In dealing with the general theory of poetry, I owe much to Professor Bradley's *Oxford Lectures on Poetry*, and to *A New Study of English Poetry* by Sir Henry Newbolt, to whom also I am grateful for his kind permission to reprint in Chapter IV. a paragraph from the book just mentioned.

It is impossible to read unstirred the Prefaces published in the present year by Mr. Thomas Hardy to *Late Lyrics and*

Earlier, and by Mr. Alfred Noyes to *The Torch-Bearers*, with their insistent call for a closer alliance between Poetry and Religion. Our religious thought to-day has much to gain from the poet's perceptions of life. Poetry, with its intuitions of the movement of life as a rhythmic whole, is a form of truth. The reconstruction of religious dogma which the present situation demands, will not mean, even if successful, that we have done with speculation. The poetic view of life—the 'Soul' of Poetry—will save us from becoming as those who, to quote Sir Walter Raleigh in his *Wordsworth*, ' fear lest the air of heaven should reach them through an unstopped chink in their creed.' The following pages, it is hoped, may help the reader to realise that the 'Soul' of modern poetry, in spite of much that is unattractive and ephemeral, loyally attempts to utter and to answer the ancient longing for a more perfect world. Our best poets to-day are not content merely to be overheard ; they desire to share their experience with their fellow-men.

R. H. STRACHAN.

EDINBURGH, 1922.

Acknowledgments

SINCERE thanks are due to the following authors and publishers who have allowed me to make partial and sometimes extensive use of copyright poems :—Mr. John Murray, for passages from the poetry of Robert Browning and some lines from the Sonnets of Mr. Robert Bridges ; Messrs. T. Fisher Unwin, a stanza from *The Lake Isle of Innisfree* (' Poems ') by Mr. W. B. Yeats ; Messrs. Sidgwick and Jackson, lines from a sonnet by Rupert Brooke, *The Volunteer* by Herbert Asquith, the poems and plays of Mr. John Drinkwater, and *The Everlasting Mercy* by Mr. John Masefield ; Mr. John Masefield himself, for permission to quote from the poem just mentioned, from *Dauber*, and from sonnets in *Lollingdon Downs* ; Messrs. John Lane, part of *Oxford from the Trenches* (' A Highland Regiment ') by E. A. Macintosh, and passages from Mr. Lascelles Abercrombie's *The End of the World* ; Mr. Gordon Bottomley, for lines from *To Ironfounders and Others* (' Chambers of Imagery,' 2nd Series, Elkin Mathews) ; Messrs. Macmillan and Co., extracts from ' Poems ' by Mr. Ralph Hodgson, ' Collected Poems ' and ' The Dynasts ' by Mr. Thomas Hardy, ' The Hill of Vision ' by Mr. James Stephens, ' Poems ' by W. E. Henley, and ' Collected Poems ' by T. E. Brown ; Messrs. Burns, Oates, and Washbourne, a passage from *The Hound of Heaven* by Francis Thompson, and from *The House of Christmas* by Mr. G. K. Chesterton ; Mr. Jonathan Cape, for an extract from *The Child and the Mariner* (' Songs of Joy ') by Mr. W. H. Davies ; Mrs. Fredegond Shove and Mr. Basil Blackwell, lines from *The New Ghost* (' Dreams and Journeys ') ; Messrs. Selwyn and Blount, some lines from *Music Comes* (' Stone Trees ') by Mr. John Freeman ; Messrs. W. Collins, Sons and Co., an extract from *The Leaning*

Elm (' Poems : 1916-1918 ') by Mr. Francis
Brett Young ; Mr. Alfred Noyes and
Messrs. W. Blackwood and Sons, the
stanza from *The Lord of Misrule* (' Collected Poems,' vol. iii.) ; Messrs. Hodder
and Stoughton, passages from the poems
of Mr. Herbert Trench ; the Trustees of
George Meredith, for various quotations
from his Poems, Miss Rose Macaulay, lines
from *New Year*, 1918 (' Three Days '),
Mr. Walter de la Mare, extracts from ' The
Listeners,' ' Motley and Other Poems,'
' The Veil and Other Poems,' and to Messrs.
Archibald Constable and Co., their publishers ; Professor Sorley, for the lines from
' Marlborough and Other Poems ' (Cam-
bridge University Press) by C. H. Sorley ;
Messrs. Chatto and Windus, passages from
' Ardours and Endurances ' by Mr. Robert
Nichols ; Lord Desborough, the stanzas
from *Into Battle* (' Soldier Poets,' Erskine
Macdonald) by the late Hon. Julian Gren-
fell, D.S.O. ; Messrs. Wm. Heinemann, the
lines from *Everyone Sang* (' War Poems ')

by Mr. Siegfried Sassoon ; Mr. Laurence Binyon, a stanza from *For the Fallen* (' The Times ') ; Sir Henry Newbolt, a stanza from *Memory* by Mary E. Coleridge.

I would also gratefully acknowledge permission granted by Messrs. Macmillan and Co. to reprint *The Mystery* by Mr. Ralph Hodgson, and *At a Lunar Eclipse* by Mr. Thomas Hardy ; and by Mr. Martin Secker to reprint *Tenebris Interlucentem* by J. E. Flecker (' Collected Poems ').

As a rule the shorter poems referred to in the text by title only, and several of those from which extracts are taken, will be found in *An Anthology of Modern Verse* by A. Methuen.

R. H. S.

Table of Contents

CHAPTER I

THE LINEAGE OF MODERN POETRY FROM WORDSWORTH TO MASEFIELD

CHAPTER II

THE MEANING OF LIFE

CHAPTER III

THE POET AS CREATOR

The sense in which poets as well as philosophers,
workers, moralists, and saints are all

CHAPTER IV

GOOD AND EVIL IN POETRY

CHAPTER V

FUTURISM AND THE SPIRIT OF REVOLT

CHAPTER VI

WAR IN MODERN POETRY

War never before so sensitively recorded in human
feeling—the new burden not only a burden

CHAPTER VII

DEATH AND IMMORTALITY

The absence of the *ripae ulterioris amor* in contemporary poetry—absence of belief in
personal survival after death to-day an
accompaniment of an idealistic, not a

THE LINEAGE OF MODERN POETRY FROM WORDSWORTH TO MASEFIELD

The objects of the Poet's thoughts are everywhere ; though the eyes and senses of man are, it is true, his favourite guides, yet he will follow wheresoever he can find an atmosphere of sensation in which to move his wings. . . . If the labours of Men of Science should ever create any material revolution, direct or indirect, in our condition, and in the impressions which we habitually receive, the Poet will sleep then no more than at present.

> WORDSWORTH, *Preface to Lyrical Ballads.*

I will arise and go now, for always night and day
I hear lake water lapping with low sounds by the
    shore ;
While I stand on the roadway, or on the pavements
    gray,
I hear it in the deep heart's core.

> W. B. YEATS, *The Lake Isle of Innisfree.*

BY Modern Poetry is meant chiefly, but not solely, the poetry published during the last twenty years.   Both George Meredith and Mr. Thomas Hardy must be included in our survey. Meredith, in many ways, as we shall see, both anticipated and shared the thought and outlook of the present century. Mr. Hardy, also, has published practically the whole of his poetry since 1898, although a great deal of it was written at a much earlier date—and even before the publication of his first novel in 1871. The absence of finality in his massive thinking commends him to the spirit of to-day. *The Dynasts*, which appeared during the period 1904-1908, only gives collective expression, under the form of a Napoleonic drama, to those ' unadjusted impressions ' of life which are embodied in his numerous lyrics. The philosophy of life which this epic drama contains is acknowledged to be tentative. The wistful longings and the bursts of lyric joy which continue to relieve his sombre philosophy have won for him, in the heart of to-day, a welcome to which his heralding of a return to the simple and direct humanism of Greek art and drama has also largely contributed.

Matthew Arnold has said that the poet is the best interpreter of his age. If this is taken to mean that the poet is peculiarly sensitive to the currents of thought, to the problems that perplex and the outward happenings that move the hearts of his contemporaries, the judgment is particularly applicable to modern poetry. It is as an extremely sensitive record of the bewildering currents and cross-currents of contemporary thought in its attitude towards life that present-day poetry is significant. We may apply to our contemporary verse a verdict passed by Professor Saintsbury on modern literature generally : it is, he says, characterised by ' a vagabond curiosity of matter, and a tormented unrest of style.' The cause must be sought largely in the conception of life which underlies and seeks expression in the poetry of to-day.

'The vagabond curiosity of matter' is really due to the claim that the world of men and of things—ever being laid bare by the discoveries of science, by the ever-deepening sensitiveness of the modern man to pain, sorrow, and death, by the increasing pace and ever-growing strenuousness and breadth of human existence—must in the end yield a universal harmony, as yet only partially perceived. Men, to-day, refuse allegiance to leaders and systems. The generalisations of the scientist, the philosopher, and the theologian in the past are found to be inadequate. The hard, clear light of scientific thought only serves to reveal that all things are in perpetual movement. Human nature breaks the bonds of logic and chooses to follow its own passionate preferences.

Mankind are not pieces—there 's your fault !
You cannot push them, and, the first move made,
Lean back and study what the next will be,
In confidence that, when 'tis fixed upon,
You find just where you left them, blacks and whites :
Men go on moving when your hand 's away.[1]

If the poet of to-day is to be an interpreter of his age, he must be able to interpret movement ; not only the unceasing movement of the external world, and of the hidden forces that propel and shake it, but those emotions of happiness, sorrow, misgiving, or longing, which are the human response to these outward impressions.

> The *movement* he must tell of life
> Its pain and pleasure, rest and strife.

The reason why the poet must ' tell ' is that we cannot utter these impressions ourselves. In all moments of joy, or sorrow, or awe, the majority of men need a new language ; otherwise they are inarticulate.

> Was never voice of ours could say
> Our inmost in the sweetest way,
> Like yonder voice aloft, and link
> All hearers in the song they drink.[2]

A similar thought is also finely expressed in Mr. Siegfried Sassoon's *Everyone Sang*, to be found in his *War Poems*. A bird sings over the trenches, and

Everyone's voice was suddenly lifted ;
And beauty came like the setting sun :
My heart was shaken with tears ; and horror
Drifted away. . . . O but Everyone
Was a bird ; and the song was wordless ; the
  singing will never be done.

We could not hear such a wordless human melody without the poet.

> Oh ! many are the Poets that are sown
> By Nature ; men endowed with highest gifts,
> The vision and the faculty divine ;
> Yet wanting the accomplishment of verse.[3]

The poet expresses what we cannot express for ourselves. Through him, as a high priest of life's mysteries, we know that we are understood, and are cheered by an answering call in the great universe. The call is more than a reverberating echo; for the poet must be regarded not merely as one who has a particular gift of words, but above all as possessing a sensitiveness of perception denied to other men.

I

The 'tormented unrest of style' in modern poetry, like its vagabond curiosity of matter, has its own origins. There are the *vers-libristes*, futurists, all the experimenters with new forms of metre and rhyme. Sometimes they represent a deliberate revolt against the tyranny of past forms, but more often their unrest of style is an attempt at outward expression in form of the bewildering variety of impressions, intuitively received, which reach men to-day out of the ordinary movement of daily life. Ours is a poetry of daily life in a sense undreamt of by Wordsworth, even in the light of his prophetic statement quoted at the beginning of the chapter. The modern poet largely refuses to subscribe to Wordsworth's definition of poetry as ' emotion recollected in tranquillity,' a conception of poetry nobly described by Sir Walter Raleigh as ' a sort of chantry, so to say, where the souls of great moments that had perished on distant fields with never a word said might be commemorated by the voice of piety.' Wordsworth's principle that the daily life of ordinary men in rustic surroundings is the true material for poetry is now interpreted to mean that the poet's material is the whole range of the ordinary and common life of men, as it is lived to-day. This wide and catholic choice of fleeting themes is seen in the attempt to utter the poetry of ' the things we live and work with ' ; also to give expression to difficult and complex passions and emotions which are generated, not in simple rustic surroundings, but amid the tumult and strain of modern social conditions. The human emotion of *The Everlasting Mercy* or of *The Widow in the Bye-Street* is not such as to the ordinary eye is ' incorporated with the beautiful and permanent forms of Nature ' ; yet they could not have found more ' direct and simple expression ' than in these two poems. Mr. Masefield has discovered more completely a truth hidden from Words-worth, that underneath the surface of apparently placid rural society there rages a war of human passion. ' Wherever there is human society there is war ; . . . Beasts fight with horns, and men, when the guns are silent, with words.' [4]   The modern poet plants his feet firmly on earth as Meredith has taught him to do, and his subjects are not so much chosen by as given to him in the real movement of life itself. The modern poetry of life is not a tinge of colour which the poet splashes on the actual, or a mood of his own in which he bathes it. In the most sincere poetry of to-day something is really given the poet which is part of the great life-urge itself. Mr. Masefield's ' cheap tin-trays,' ' road-rails,' and ' pig-lead ' in *Cargoes* are really sources and suggestions of emotion to the poet. He thinks of those by whose toil they are produced, as in *Dauber* :—

> Thus is bread fetched and ports won
> And life lived out at sea where men exist
> Solely by man's strong brain and sturdy wrist.

At the same time, the wide range of contemporary poetry is not entirely inconsistent with Wordsworth's vision. ' If the time should ever come,' says Wordsworth, 'when what is now called science, thus familiarised to men, shall be ready to put on, as it were, a form of flesh and blood, the Poet will lend his divine spirit to aid the transfiguration, and will welcome the Being thus produced, as a dear and genuine inmate of the household of man.' Wordsworth carried into his idea of the function of poetry a prophetic breadth of view, which the poet of to-day claims as his own.

Aristotle laid it down long ago, as a first principle of tragedy, that the central character should be ' one of high fame,' belonging to an illustrious family, like Oedipus or Thyestes. Dr. Johnson once said in conversation with Boswell, ' When a butcher tells you that *his heart bleeds for his country,* he has in fact no uneasy feeling.' The assumption is that such hearts are never so deeply moved. Wordsworth represented a historic reaction against this doctrine when he laid it down, that in the simple life of the countryman there are to be found real lyric or tragic elements, great in their simplicity. To Robert Burns, he owned, was due his earliest vision of this revolutionary truth—

> How Verse may build a princely throne
> On humble truth.

Ordinary men and women can experience great emotions of sacrifice and patriotism, of love and hate, of joy and sorrow. They show and they are moved by kindness. They can be great in courage, in endurance, in hope. They have moments of profound despair. A sunrise, a garden, a mountain, or a flower can speak to them. In wife, or husband, or child, they also give hostages to fortune.

Wordsworth's claim for rural humanity, however, was not due to mere class-sympathy; nor was his direct intention to glorify the humble labourer. He began by asking, ' Where can I see, and get others to see, ordinary human nature, when moved, at its best ? What is the most favourable situation in which the poet may best describe human perception of things as they are ? ' The sublimity and endurance shown in the life of the humble country toiler, Wordsworth ascribed to the influence of ' the natural objects to which men were linked by many associations.' This doubtless is an illustration of the truth that ' Wordsworth sees Nature first, and Man afterwards.' In his poetry, Man is often but an aspect of natural scenery. His pedlars, leech-gatherers, and village-dwellers are ' the stately nobles of Nature,' with something of the magnificence of the hills, the peace of the valleys, the purity of the bubbling spring, interfused in their characters.

Wordsworth's method of dealing with the themes suggested to him in daily life is strikingly illustrated in the following quotation from the journal of Dorothy Wordsworth. This account is given of the incident which gave rise to the poem *Resolution and Independence.* ' We met an old man almost double. He had a coat thrown over his shoulders . . . under this he carried a bundle and had an apron on and a night-cap. His face was interesting. . . . His trade was to gather leeches, but now leeches were scarce, and he had not strength for it. He lived by begging. He said leeches were scarce, partly because of the dry season ; but many years they had been scarce. He supposed it was owing to their being sought after, that they did not breed fast, and were of slow growth. Leeches were formerly 2s. 6d. the 100, now they were 30s.' Professor E. de Sélincourt, in his *The Study of Poetry*, points out that Wordsworth omits ' the apron, the night-cap, and the statistics.' The man is not associated with the road on which he had actually met him, but is placed beside a mountain-pool on a lonely moor. The alteration in the setting is significant of one important difference between Wordsworth and the modern poet. A ' Georgian ' poet would probably make no such alteration, and would no doubt include apron, night-cap, and even the statistics ! Modern poetry refuses to look on man as an aspect of Nature. The sublimity, pathos, and endurance of humanity are inherent, and not reflected qualities. They are as native to human character as those less comely qualities which Wordsworth suppresses. In view of Mr. Masefield's *Saul Kane* or his *Widow in the Bye-Street* it is strange to read Wordsworth's frank confession regarding his characters, that their language ' has been purified from what appears to be its natural defects, from all lasting and rational causes of dislike and disgust.'

The drift of population from the country to the city has left its mark on our modern verse. Attention may be called to such a poem as Mr. Harold Monro's *Man carrying Bale*. Mr. Drinkwater's lines in *From a Town Window* are also typical of the change :—

> Under the grey drift of the town
>   The crocus works among the mould
> As eagerly as those that crown
>   The Warwick spring in flame and gold.
>
> And when the tramway down the hill
>   Across the cobbles moans and rings,
> There is about my window-sill
>   The tumult of a thousand wings.[5]

Wordsworth's muse is never at home in the life of the city, and sings most easily of the city ' asleep ' in the early morning when

> All that mighty heart is lying still.

The growth of industrial conditions, the increased struggle for wealth and livelihood seem to baffle Wordsworth as a poet. In his later days, the advance of science and the growing revelation of Nature's secrets, inviting men to all kinds of intellectual experiments—scientific, philosophical, religious—and producing manifold misgiving in the heart of man, are accepted with a calm faith, but the life of the city distracted his senses and laid ' the whole creative powers of man asleep.' In his famous Preface he speaks of the mind of man as reduced in cities to ' a state of almost savage torpor,' which gives rise to ' a craving for extraordinary incident,' and ' a degrading thirst after outrageous stimulation.' He speaks of

that pent-up-din,
Those life-consuming sounds that clog the air ;

and

the fierce confederate storm
Of sorrow barricadoed evermore
Within the walls of cities.

Life in cities is unfriendly to poetry :—

> The world is too much with us ; late and soon,
> Getting and spending, we lay waste our powers ;
> Little we see in Nature that is ours ;
> We have given our hearts away, a sordid boon !

Wordsworth, however, built far bigger than he knew, and his return to common life as providing subjects for poetry was the signal for the beginning of a movement which culminates in the present wide range of poetical theme, with all its vagaries and eccentricities.   At the same time, it would be a mistake to attribute to Wordsworth a dislike of all but well-regulated and restrained expression of emotional experience.   His specific objection to ' the accumulation of men in cities ' is that it leads to ' torpor ' of soul.   Whether his judgment be right or wrong, apparently his chief enemy is ' torpor ' wherever he finds it.[6]   He complains that statesmen, in elaborating measures for the relief and

abolition of poverty, would sweep away
his old Cumberland Beggar.

> Ye
> Who have a broom still ready in your hands
> To rid the world of nuisances.

Professor Bradley is no doubt correct in
his surmise, that Wordsworth's only objection to the beggar's disappearance is not
that he is ' a silent monitor,' and exists
in order that

> the kindly mood in hearts
> May be kept alive.

With some confidence it may be said that
his most powerful objection to the pro-
posed reforms was that statesmen were
blind to the real dignity of human nature
displayed in the free unconventional life
of the beggar.   Wordsworth deeply appre-
ciates the difference between the spon-
taneous giving of humble generous souls
in obedience to kindly instinct, and ' these

inevitable charities.' He also loves the old man because in his continual wandering he presents a picture of one who must often brave the elements—

> let his blood
> Struggle with frosty air and winter snows ;
> And let the chartered wind that sweeps the heath
> Beat his gray locks against his withered face.

The Cumberland Beggar is no portrait of hopeless, passive submission. Here is the old original subject of all tragedy, but he need not be ' one of high fame.' The beggar's staff is in imagination exchanged for a sceptre. He might be Oedipus or Orestes, equally an example of

> the dread strife
> Of pure humanity's afflicted will
> Struggling in vain with ruthless destiny.

Even *Alice Fell* has been thus finely interpreted by that convinced Wordsworthian, Professor Bradley. Alice, crying for the loss of her cloak, is ' a child who has an imagination, and who sees the tattered remnants of her cloak whirling in the wheel-spokes of a post-chaise fiercely driven by strangers on lonesome roads through a night of storm in which the moon is drowned.' [7] On the other hand, Wordsworth, in contrast with the modern poet, is hampered by his doctrine of ' emotion recollected in tranquillity.' He admits that the poet's expression must fall short ' in liveliness and truth ' of the experience of men in real life ' under the actual pressure of those passions.' His representation, in other words, is shrouded in a mist of contemplative feeling, which springs from his own heart. In his view this mood of contemplation is the medium through which alone it is permissible to present the real action and suffering of men, and their passion thus becomes neither ' harsh ' nor ' grating ' but ' the still sad music of humanity.' Here there emerges one chief point of controversy between the champions of the old and the supporters of the newer school of poetry.

II

In the attempt to trace from Wordsworth the lineal descent of the general spirit and outlook (apart from the form) of twentieth-century poetry, it becomes fairly clear that, if we pass over the influence of Shelley and Keats, which is comparatively slight, and leave out in the meantime Browning and Tennyson, against both of whom modern poetic thought is in reaction, George Meredith is the next great formative influence. Meredith and Wordsworth alike regard Nature and Man as ' essentially adapted to one another.' Meredith, however, has clearly recognised that all men do not live their lives as ' mirrors of the fairest and most interesting

properties of Nature.' Meredith, as, for
example, in *The Woods of Westermain,*
brings into prominence the darker element
in Nature, which to Wordsworth was
clearly present but was much more an
intellectual than a moral burden—

> The heavy and the weary weight
> Of all this unintelligible world.

In a faith fostered by Nature's prevailing
mood, her ' quietness and beauty,' he will
not allow disturbance to

> Our cheerful faith, that all which we behold
> Is full of blessings.

He reads in the faces of the clouds ' un-
utterable blessings,' and among the mountains all things ' breathe immortality.'
Meredith, on the other hand, stresses
Nature's darker side. In one of her
aspects, Nature is out to hawk, a hooded
falcon :—

> Thousand eyeballs under hoods
> Have you by the hair.

The adaptation of Man to Nature is for
Meredith a courageous achievement of man
himself, and not a gift of the gods. Nature
teaches, not only in contemplation, but
by blows, ' thwackings,' and she teaches
courage :—

> But should you distrust a tone,
>   Then beware.
> Shudder all the haunted roods,
> All the eyeballs under hoods
>   Shroud you in their glare.
> Enter these enchanted woods,
>   You who dare.[8]

We may, like Wordsworth, turn to rural
nature for inspiration and strength, but it
is amid other surroundings than mountains
and streams that the greater part of our
life is lived. We are children of ' Earth,'
and ' Earth ' includes not only the
country but the town, both forest and
city. Meredith, as we know, will have
nothing to do with immortality, nor with

those obstinate questionings that are directed towards the management of the universe, and seem to proclaim that Earth is not our home. Earth is our ' mother.'

Meredith can see no goal towards which civilisation is moving, save man himself. Men, individually, are creatures of a day ; the aim is that as the generations of men succeed one another, an ever higher and more spiritual type of the human race should be evolved. This higher human type is not merely fostered by Earth, but is actually the product of ' mother-earth.' In Wordsworth, Earth is only man's foster-mother, and ' our birth is but a sleep and a forgetting ' :—

> The homely nurse doth all she can
> To make her foster-child, her inmate, Man,
>> Forget the glories he hath known
> And that imperial palace whence he came.

In Meredith, man is ' Earth's greatest venture.' Man himself must co-operate, and must take his own share in the struggle. Man is Nature's crown and flower. The growth of modern civilisation in towns and cities is not a backward step in man's development, with all its ruthlessness towards human life. There indeed ' our battle urges,' and the struggle is at its height ; thence also spring ' those warriors of the sighting brain,' leaders in thought and statesmanship, art and commerce, who renew the youth of worn humanity.[9] The concourse of men in cities does not mean, as Plato would have had it, the expulsion of the poet. In his view the life of country and city alike yield material for the poet. The ' sighting brain ' is the organ of the ' soul ' ; it accepts what Nature originally decreed should be the laws of our being. It is neither sensual nor ascetic. Nature's laws are plain for all to read, and stimulating to those who accept them. This acceptance of the doctrines of evolutionary science is the condition of the soul's growth.   The poet is of those

> Who see in mould the rose unfold,
> The soul through blood and tears.[10]

The vision of beauty demands courage. ' Earth's secret ' is to be found neither in ' field ' nor in ' turbid city ' taken by itself. The key is in the hands of those ' hither, thither fare,' those to whom, in other words, the whole of life is open and congenial.   Meredith has taught men to face facts in a spirit of catholic understanding and dauntless courage.   ' The Woods of Westermain ' are a symbol of life, and life demands, above all, courage.

> Enter these enchanted woods
> Ye who dare.

III

The poet of to-day, with all his bewildering catholicity of theme and his equally bewildering variety of expression, is certainly of those who ' hither, thither fare.' The difficulty immediately confronts us how to treat in any systematic fashion the thought that is expressed in such an amazing variety of forms as we find in modern poetry. To speak generally, the aim of the modern poet is still the ancient quest for beauty, order, harmony in life. He conducts it with a pertinacity that refuses to be daunted, no matter how ugly, painful, and miserable that life may be.   He has, for the most part, duly accepted Meredith's teaching that ' Earth is our only visible friend,' but he is not disposed to accept Meredith's theory that Nature's ' thwackings,' the sinister chances and changes of life, are a wise discipline meant to enable us to accept her ways and to live according to her creative purpose. He has caught the spirit of Meredith's optimism—or to use his own ugly word, his ' meliorism.' Things are somehow getting better. Life, however, is, as William James says, in *The Will to Believe*, ' an unfinished fight :—

It feels like a real fight,—as if there were something really wild in the universe which we, with all our individualities and faithfulnesses, are needed to redeem ; and first of all to redeem our own souls from atheisms and fears.

It is not without significance, in view of the prevailing philosophy, that in Mr. Masefield's *Dauber* the artistic passion, in *The Widow in the Bye-Street* a mother's affection, in *The Everlasting Mercy* the soul's struggle with sense, should each emerge triumphantly from the fierce fight with circumstance and evil. The same idea may be traced in *Reynard the Fox*, in form and expression the finest of his narrative work. Mr. Drinkwater's portrait of Abraham Lincoln as ' the lord of his event ' has made a noble and successful appeal to the popular spirit. Beauty is conceived as courageous achievement, and there can be no ultimate harmony without moral victory in this sense. Poetry of this kind is in reaction against a weak aestheticism, and marks a return to the original Hellenic conception of beauty. The Greek was interested in life first and in art second, and held that it was a better thing for a man to enact the drama of life than to see it on the stage.[11] This conception of Beauty as a courageous achievement is encountered even in poets who have chosen themes with much less dramatic possibility than those of Mr. Masefield or Mr. Drinkwater. Even Mr. de la Mare, whose real world seems to be a dream-world of elusive beauty, beyond or beneath the world of sense, in which the poet is ' the one man left awake,' has in *The Listeners* described the poetic quest under the figure of a traveller on horseback, who dismounts at the 'moonlit door' of a mysterious house in the midst of a forest. He knocks at the door repeatedly, demanding entrance into the hidden world of beauty. Silence is his answer, but we are made to feel that the house is inhabited :—

A host of phantom listeners
That dwelt in the lone house then
Stood listening in the quiet of the moonlight
To that voice from the world of men :
Stood thronging the faint moonbeams on the dark
    stair,
That goes down to the empty hall,
Hearkening in an air stirred and shaken
By the lonely Traveller's call.

In his later volume *The Veil and Other Poems,* Mr. de la Mare has achieved this courageous type of beauty in uglier material than that in which he has hitherto worked, as, for example, in *In the Dock, The Suicide,* and *Drugged.*

IV

It is difficult to assign Mr. Thomas Hardy his place in the historic succession. In the Preface to his latest volume, *Late Lyrics and Earlier*, he dissociates himself from the present-day tendencies in poetry. His judgment on modern poetry is somewhat surprising, inasmuch as one is disposed to think of Mr. Hardy as himself grown grey, though never old, in serving a conception of poetry applied to common life, akin to that of the moderns, who have as yet achieved far less noble and profound results. That conception is impressionist. Mr. Hardy, in the same Preface, describes his own ' view ' of life as a ' series of fugitive impressions which I have never tried to co-ordinate ' ; elsewhere he has called it a ' series of unadjusted impressions.' He acknowledges Matthew Arnold's definition of poetry—the application of ideas to life, by which I suppose is meant that poetry is an emotional reasoning about life. It seems to the present writer that it is precisely the theory that poetry may consist in unadjusted and fugitive impressions of life, that forms the link between Mr. Hardy and a great deal of our modern poetry. Moreover, he, too, is in opposition to the aristocratic view of tragedy that the fates of kings, princes, or prelates are alone the proper subjects for poetic treatment. He is at one with Mr. Masefield when the latter says in *Consecration* :—

Of the maimed, of the halt and the blind in the rain
    and the cold—
Of these shall my songs be fashioned, my tale be told.

In the *Dynasts*, his view clearly is, that what happens to Napoleon when his star is set is also what has happened to the countless corpses that strew the battlefield of Waterloo, or mark the disastrous retreat from Moscow. The same thing even has happened to the rabbits that flee, scared by the thud of the hoofs, or in ' the mole's tunnelled chambers' crushed by the cannon-wheels, to the lark whose eggs are scattered, the snail crushed by the passing limbers, the worm and the trodden and bruised herbage :—

> And each soul shivers as sinks his head
> On the loam he 's to lease with the other dead.[12]

The same destiny overwhelms the humblest of human lives, as Tess the dairymaid who slays her lover, and lies under sentence of death, and any of those lovers in his poems so ' hopelessly wed ' or ' haplessly jilted,' as one of his critics has aptly described them. In the *Dynasts* there is conceived on a grand scale, with great historical figures as actors—it is hard to say often whether they are active or passive, moved or moving—what is happening in countless human lives. Destiny is simply to give the activity a name, but to tell nothing of its character. It is not so much an activity, as Mr. Lascelles Abercrombie says, as a condition of activity.

In his poem *Afterwards*, Mr. Hardy describes the working of his own poetic mind. The refrain of the poem is 'He used to notice such things.' He speaks as a poet of Nature—of the coming of the leaf in spring, the dewfall-hawk alighting on 'the wind-warped upland thorn,' the hedgehog travelling 'furtively over the lawn,' the mystery of 'the full-starred heavens that winter sees,' the crossing breeze that 'cuts a pause' in the tones of a bell

Till they rise again, as they were a new bell's boom.

Is he not, however, much more the poet of Man, and does he not share to the full what Ruskin calls ' the pathetic fallacy,' that Nature is the witness and *confidante* of Man's inmost thought, and shares his joy and his sorrow ?   Hamlets, single farms, coombs, single trees in his beloved Wessex are known to him intimately ; but he knows them chiefly for certain tales of human tragedy and sorrow connected with them.   He constantly connects places and people.   Nature, for him, does not dominate as in Wordsworth, but exists only to suggest memories of men and women long dead, and to utter the poet's own thoughts. Compare the lines from *Beyond the Last Lamp* :—

> Without those comrades there at tryst
>   Creeping slowly, creeping sadly,
>   That lone lane does not exist.
> There they seem brooding on their pain,
> And will, while such a lane remain.

Modern poetry owes much both to Meredith and to Mr. Hardy—to Meredith a legacy of indomitable courage, ' the warrior heart,' to Mr. Hardy the scientific spirit which closely observes the truth about human life as it glances

Across the shadowed tracks of fate and chance.

Meredith's faith is the faith of the Stoic, who recognises the distinction between the things that are and the things that are not ' within our power ' to alter or to understand. Mr. Hardy's faith issues in constant protest against the suppression of individual instinct, whether of reason or of feeling. Even while he speaks of destiny and fate, he protests that ' feeling ' and ' puppetry ' are incompatible. He does not resign himself to the inevitableness of man's earthly fortune. He speaks of it too sadly or even too savagely for that. He would not acquiesce as Meredith does in the position that man must be his own redeemer. Mr. Hardy does not yet see

on the horizon the feet of the heralds that
bring good tidings to the besieged city of
Mansoul, but he looks for them eagerly :—

> Yet I would bear my shortcomings
>   With meet tranquillity,
> But for the charge that blessed things
>   I 'd liefer not have be.
> O doth a bird deprived of wings
>   Go earth-bound wilfully ! [13]

nor would he reconcile himself to Meredith's
utterance :—

> No extra-mural God, the God within
> Alone gives aid to the city charged with sin.[14]

Mr. Hardy's poetry ranks as it does,
inasmuch as it keeps alive that hunger for
reality, and that sense of homelessness on
earth, which is native to man's spirit. Our
best modern poetry is filled with a sense
of home-sickness which continually breaks
through the bonds that doom men to
acquiescence in things as they are.   It

appears as a continual quest for beauty, and a continual welcoming of it as it appears ' in the stream of lovely things—the stream that flows and yet remains.' [15] The poet is animated by the same daring and imaginative faith which possessed the soul of the Hebrew poet and prophet, who, looking upon waterless Jerusalem, yet exclaimed, ' Lo ! a river, the streams whereof make glad the city of our God.'

V

In Mr. G. K. Chesterton's *The House of Christmas*, the lines occur :—

> The world is wild as an old wives' tale,
>   And strange the plain things are,
> The earth is enough and the air is enough
>   For our wonder and our war.

If we were seeking for a generalisation in which might be summed up the intellectual characteristics of contemporary poetry we

might borrow a phrase from Mr. Chesterton
and call it the poetry of wonder and of
war—of the wonder and mystery that
pervades the work of poets like Mr. de la
Mare or Mr. W. H. Davies (in such a poem
as *A Great Time*), or of the victorious war
with evil and circumstance—' the elements
of this world ' in Pauline phrase — that
characterises, say, Mr. Masefield's work.
Take, for example, the passage in *Dauber*,
where he describes the birth of Dauber's
artistic vocation amid all the turmoil and
danger of a storm at sea :—

A thought occurred
Within the poet's brain like a bright bird :
That this, and so much like it, of man's toil,
Compassed by naked manhood in strange places,
Was all heroic, but outside the coil
Within which modern art gleams or grimaces ;
That if he drew that line of sailor's faces
Sweating the sail, their passionate play and change,
It would be new, and wonderful, and strange :

That that was what his work meant ; it would be
A training in new vision—a revealing
Of passionate men in battle with the sea,
High on an unseen stage, shaking and reeling ;
And men through him would understand their
    feeling,
Their might, their misery, their tragic power,
And all by suffering pain a little hour.[16]

The same note is heard in the opening lines of Mr. Drinkwater's *Abraham
Lincoln* :—

> This is the wonder, always, everywhere—
> Not that vast mutability which is event,
> The pits and pinnacles of change,
> But man's desire and valiance that range
> All circumstance, and come to port unspent.

There is also the poetry of ' wonder.'
In Mr. de la Mare's work, this nostalgic
quest for beauty and permanence utters
itself more quietly and more elusively, as
in *Haunted*. Death is the ' quiet enemy.'
Sometimes in his more recent work we

hear a more urgent cry that is reminiscent
of Thomas Hardy :—

> Cast from that Ark of Heaven which is Thy home
> The raven of hell may wander without fear ;
> But sadly wings the dove o'er floods to roam,
> Nought but one tender sprig his eyes to cheer.
> Nay, Lord, I speak in parables.   But see !
> 'Tis stricken Man in Men that pleads with Thee.[17]

Mr. de la Mare's world is surrounded
by mysterious, unseen ' Listeners.'   Their
presence is felt not only in the dark and
twilight of life, but also—and this is his
great achievement—in the clear light of
day with all that it reveals : in *A Sunken
Garden*, and *In the Dock*, where a criminal
is being tried for his life :—

> Justice for carrion pants ; and these the flies.
> Voice after voice in smooth impartial drone
> Erects horrific in his darkening brain
> A timber framework, where agape, alone
> Bright life will kiss good-bye the cheek of Cain
> Sudden like wolf he cries ; and sweats to see
> When howls man's soul, it howls inaudibly.[18]

THE MEANING OF LIFE

If this life be not a real fight, in which something is
eternally gained for the universe by success, it is
no better than a game of private theatricals from
which one may withdraw at will.

WILLIAM JAMES, *The Will to Believe*.

> This world is unto God a work of art
> Of which the unaccomplish'd heavenly plan
> Is hid in life within the creature's heart,
> And for perfection looketh unto man.

ROBERT BRIDGES, *Sonnet XVI*.

A DEFINITION of poetry is hard to come by.
We are far better able to define what
poetry does than what poetry is. Sir
Henry Newbolt has said that the criterion
of great poetry is that it ' touches the
universal longing for a perfect world.' [1]
Meanwhile we may pass by the question
whether there are any ' great ' poets to-day.
It is far more profitable to seek for great

poetry than for great poets ; for it is not the man who makes his poetry great, but the opposite. If Sir Henry Newbolt is right in his test, our search will not be in vain. This universal longing for a perfect world reappears to-day, as strongly as in any other age of poetry. It is true that poets utter it, not as they lift up their eyes to the hills, but as they stand on the roadway of a great city, all the bustle and roar of its movement in their ears, or tread its ' pavements grey.' [2] The poets are men and women haunted by sights and sounds which, to ordinary mortals, are but darkness and silence ; see-ers and listeners without whom we would still be blind and deaf.

Poetry and not the Witch of Endor, Imagination not Reason, Intuition not Logic, to-day ' storm the secret beauty of the world.' Poetry and Religion are already preparing themselves for the renewal of an alliance which is very old, and was strong both in New Testament times and at the Reformation. Poetry has an interpretative and not merely a decorative function in life. She is Life itself, enabling us ever here and now to

Learn all we lacked before ; hear, know, and say
    What this tumultuous body now denies ;
And feel, who have laid our groping hands away,
    And see, no longer blinded by our eyes.[3]

The longing for the ' Lake Isle of Innisfree ' is the fruit of no mere despair of life as it is, no narcotic administered to the wakeful spirit of man. On the contrary, the poet is, as Mr. de la Mare describes him, ' the one man left awake.' The poet is a traveller whose knocking on the door of the mysterious unseen world, and whose voice demanding entry, sound not in a tenantless void, but in an air so real and so sensitive that it can be ' stirred and shaken.' The unseen perfect world for which we long is a reality, and the home-sickness is not for a home that does not exist. The essence of all real religion, and particularly of Christianity, is that nothing that is supremely desirable or valuable to the heart of man ever perishes out of the world. The poet at least keeps alive that desire by his imaginative expression of it, and makes more credible the underlying and animating desire of all religious experience.

What is the conception of Life that animates this faith in the ultimate reality of the poetic world ? This ' poor, mortal longingness ' of ours, is it like the angel to whom Matthew Arnold—no doubt mis-takenly—compared Shelley, ' a beautiful *and ineffectual* angel, beating in the void his luminous wings in vain ' ? Does poetry make a real contribution towards an answer to the fundamental questions—

Where are we ?   What are we ?   Whither
do we go ?   Or is any satisfying answer to
these questions to be left to the philosopher ?   Does the poet set free within us
an impulse towards, and an assurance of a
perfect state of things ?   Is poetry really
the highest form of truth ?   Is the power
of song a signal that life is at least within
sight of its goal ?   Has the poet seen the
walls of a city that hath foundations ?

What does it all mean, poet ?   Well,
Your brain 's beat into rhythm, you tell
What we felt only ; you expressed
You hold things beautiful the best,

   And pace them in rhyme so, side by side.
'Tis something, nay 'tis much : but then,
Have you yourself what 's best for men ?
Are you—poor, sick, old ere your time—
Nearer one whit your own sublime
Than we who never have turned a rhyme ?
Sing, riding 's a joy !   For me, I ride.[4]

I

What is the essential difference between the view of life's meaning which we find in, say, Browning, and that which is discovered in contemporary poetry ? The lines above are taken from a poem in which Browning sings of unrequited love. It is, at the same time, a symbol of Browning's philosophy of life, which always demands ' a life beyond ' in order to complete our imperfect and unrealised life here on earth.

Heaven and she are beyond this ride.

Somewhere there exists a perfect edition of the world, a perfect edition of the individual life :—

On the earth, the broken arcs ; in the heaven, a perfect round.

Browning's theory of life is too well known to need detailed exposition, even if that were possible here. I refer to it only in order to point a contrast between it and the conception of life which dominates the thought of modern poetry. Browning's philosophy of life is speculative and metaphysical : the modern view, which comes to its best-known philosophical expression in the work of Professor Henri Bergson, is empirical. For Browning life is already a rational whole :—

> God 's in his heaven,
> All 's right with the world ;

but man is constitutionally bounded by limitations. These limitations of sense and will inevitably involve intellectual and moral failure ; but the very failure is the promise of ultimate success :—

> Why rushed the discords in, but that harmony
> should be prized ?

Browning accepts the moral and intellectual limitations of life. We must work within these, even while we see beyond, often with the eye of artist or prophet, the land of our desire.   We work in chains and long for freedom, and 'the battle between the infinite destiny of the soul and the baffling of its effort to realise its infinitude on earth makes the storm and misery of life.'[5]   The thought finds its best-known expression in *Rabbi Ben Ezra.* There Browning makes use of the austere and transcendent conception of the clay and the potter.   The soul is as clay on the potter's wheel, and the Divine Providence uses circumstance as a machinery that moulds the soul.   The finished cup will one day be set to the Master's own lips to slake His thirst :—

Look not thou down, but up !
To uses of a cup,
The festal board, lamp's flash and trumpet's peal
The new wine's foaming flow,
The Master's lips a-glow !
Thou, heaven's consummate cup, what need'st thou
       with earth's wheel ?

Our life on earth is a set of ' plastic circumstance '—that is circumstance that is expressive and not meaningless—around and within which God moves and works in order to fashion the individual life to His plan. This view of life as a training-ground for or the vestibule of a life beyond is essentially a form of what William James calls ' the tender-minded ' view of the universe, the view of those whom a deep sensitiveness to life's incompleteness urges to find their joy in the thought of a completeness above or beyond it. These

> Fix perfect homes in the unsubstantial sky
> And say what is not, shall be bye and bye.

This ' tender-minded ' view of life is that against which Meredith is in continual protest :—

> Not till the fire is dying in the grate
> Look we for any kinship with the stars.[6]

I have described this ' tender-minded '

conception of life, as it is bodied forth in a religious form in *Rabbi Ben Ezra*. It may of course take more purely philosophic form, as faith in an eternal world of truth ; or it may take an artistic form, as faith in an eternal world of Beauty—a world even now existent, where all error, and all ugliness are seen to be but parts of one great rational whole. It is bad in parts, but good as a whole ; in other words, this is the best of all possible worlds. The evil appears as nothing in comparison with the good. This ' tender-minded ' view of life is ' far less an account of this actual world,' says William James, ' than a clear addition built upon it, a classic sanctuary in which the rationalist fancy may take refuge from the intolerably confused and gothic character which mere facts present. It is no *explanation* of our concrete universe, it is another thing altogether, a substitute for it, a remedy, a way of escape.' [7]

No account of our present world, but 'a clear addition built upon it'! Is Browning's perfect world for which he longs, after all, an intellectual construction, the fruit of a rationalistic temper, both an inference from and an escape out of the concrete facts of existence? Is it that entry is effected for a light supposed to come from without, rather than the opening out a way, as Paracelsus seeks to do, 'whence the imprisoned splendour may escape'—the imprisoned splendour of our own experience, which refuses to acquiesce even in its divinely appointed limitations, and demands the opening of the prison here and now to them that are bound and liberty to them that are bruised. Even Browning, in his later work, in a short poem written probably after the death of his wife, seems to demand in his perfect world some return to the dear concrete facts of existence here :—

Others may need new life in Heaven—
  Man, Nature, Art—made new, assume !

.   .   .   .   .   .

I shall pray : 'Fugitive as precious—
  Minutes which passed,—return, remain !
Let earth's old life once more enmesh us.' [8]

It is significant that in this poem, ' earth's wheel,' all the tangled, painful, and perplexed experiences of this present world enter into the eternal substance of the perfect world. Without them it would be cold and undesirable and therefore imperfect. It would seem that even in such concrete moments of ' earth's old life ' man even now has ' forever.'

II

The question of the place of the individual in life is to-day raised with fresh urgency. He does not seek an escape from life, in the prospect of ultimate entry into a perfect world which is already in existence in the mind of God, or of the Absolute, according as we speak in terms of religion or of philosophy. Man seeks the freedom of escape *into* life. He demands not only that life should mould him, but that he also should help to mould life; that he also should have a part in conscious control of the mechanism of life. He seeks expression and recognition of an inherent creative activity of his own. Life, it is asserted, is not an evolution which is like the uncoiling of a rope, but an activity in which the individual himself is capable of bringing to bear creative energy; both by releasing an energy imprisoned in the concrete facts of life, which is waiting for release, and by himself making an addition to that energy. He is capable not only of receiving, but, as Bergson puts it, of giving more than he has, of drawing from himself more than he contains. He is a fellow-labourer with

God. The thought is similar to that in the lines quoted at the beginning of the chapter from Mr. Bridges' Sonnet XVI.

In contrast to the ' tender-minded ' view of life, this—to borrow again William James's phraseology — is the ' tough-minded ' point of view. It is the protest of humanity against the dominant idea of evolution as a mere mechanical struggle for existence, even under the guidance of a watchful Providence. Humanity accepts the principle of evolution, but repudiates the notion that the individual is only being evolved. From the religious point of view, it dissents from the notion that Providence is solely a power which, as Meredith says, ' observes and provides for the movements of creatures in the dark.' Humanity claims the right to be not merely the evolved, but also an evolver : not merely to be created, but to be a fellow-creator. What we know and feel and will is itself an addition to reality. Professor Bergson's formula of ' Creative Evolution ' is that which best sums up the conception of life and of the world which emerges in the artistic and poetic expression of our day.

Mr. Lascelles Abercrombie, who, among all our modern poets, shows leading capacity for philosophical insight, has written a remarkable short play entitled *The End of the World*. He has therein stated with clearness and precision of thought the modern position regarding the meaning of life. The general theme of the play is the effect of a rumour of the approaching end of the world, caused by the sudden appearance of a comet, on a variety of ordinary village characters. Among them is one who has been wronged in his home life, and also the man who has wronged him. Others are two artisans, a wainwright, Sollers, who has expressed his soul in his work—

> like a man sworn to a thing
> Working to have my wains in every curve,
> Ay, every tenon, right and as they should be ;

and a blacksmith, Merrick—

> the man
> Who hammers a meaning into red-hot iron.

The significance of the play is the fashion in which the consciences of the various characters react upon the ominous news. The man who has been wronged sees in the approaching catastrophe the certainty of moral vindication and of judgment on the man who has done the wrong. The guilty man, through fear, is driven to restore the woman to her husband. Homage is thus offered in both cases to conventional morality. Huff's desire, however, for judgment is discovered to be but the sour jealousy of a man who is himself too timid to do wrong, while the momentary repentance of Shale, his injurer, after the comet has passed and the coming dread is removed, is revealed as a passing mood and the offspring of terror.

The play is evidently intended to be a satire on conventional morality based on the sanction of a conventional religious outlook, which involves that the present world of concrete experiences must one day be destroyed in the interests of a higher kind of existence. Says Huff, the representative of conventional morality in the play :—

> how should I not believe a thing
> That calls aloud on my mind and spirit, and they
> Answer to it like starving conquering soldiers
> Told to break out and loot ?

Yet this attitude towards a present world ' grown gray with the breath ' of a conventional and selfish morality, fails to satisfy even the heart of the ' good ' man.

> My good life !
> And what good has my goodness been to me ?
> You show me that !   Somebody show me that !
> A caterpillar munching a cabbage-heart.

Always drudging further and further from
The sounds and lights of the World, never abroad
Nor flying free in warmth and air sweet-smelling.
A crawling caterpillar, eating his life
In a deaf dark—that 's my gain of goodness !

Mr. Abercrombie seems to have put his own philosophy of life into the mouth of Sollers the wainwright and Merrick the blacksmith. He has apparently banished the scientific and religious dogmas which demand that

Life that has done such wonders with its thinking

shall one day be

All blotcht out by a brutal thrust of fire
Like a midge that a clumsy thumb squashes and
smears,

He is, like Rupert Brooke, a ' Great Lover ' of the actual things that delight the senses :—

I was delighted with my life : there seemed
Naught but things to enjoy.   Say we were bathing :
There 'ld be the cool smell of the water, and cool
The splashing under the trees.

Life, however, is no mad plunge into grossness :—

> I did loathe
> The sinking mud slithering round my feet,
> And I did love to loathe it so !

Like Meredith, he would have us speed our way between ' the ascetic rocks and the sensual whirlpools.' [9] Earth indicates more than happiness ; our aim is to be fellow-creatures of the ultimate creative power :—

> ' You know, this is much more than being happy.
> 'Tis hunger of some power in you, that lives
> On your heart's welcome for all sorts of luck,
> But always looks beyond you for its meaning.'
> And that 's the way the world 's kept going on,
> I believe now.   Misery and delight
> Have both had liking welcome from it, both
> Have made the world keen to be glad and sorry.
> For why ?   It felt the living power thrive
> The more it made everything, good and bad,
> Its own belonging, forged to its own affair,—
> The living power that would do wonders some day.

The business of the artist, whatever his material, is to keep alive

at its best

The skill that must go forward and shape the world,
Helping it on to make some masterpiece.

It is an application of Ruskin's great teaching about labour, which is itself derived from a teaching still nobler, and affording a clearer indication of the character of the Power that animates all life : ' Raise the stone, and there thou shalt find me ; cleave the wood, and there am I.'

III

The real function of poetry in the conduct of life was described long ago by Shelley in his *Defence of Poetry*. In one passage of his essay he speaks of poetry as the divine creative faculty which enables us to imagine what we already know, and supplies the generous impulse to act that which we imagine. ' The cultivation of those sciences which have enlarged the limits of the empire of man over the external world, has, for want of the poetical faculty, proportionally circumscribed those of the internal world ; and man, having enslaved the elements, remains himself a slave.' He passes a judgment on the social conditions of his own day, which might equally well be applied to our own. These are often reflected in the work of modern poets, such as Mr. W. W. Gibson or Wilfrid Owen. The mechanical arts, says Shelley, ' have been cultivated in a degree disproportioned to the presence of the creative faculty. . . . From what other cause has it arisen that the discoveries which should have lightened, have added a weight to the curse imposed on Adam ? Poetry, and the principle of self, of which money is the visible incarnation, are the God and Mammon of the world.' Our souls have become too small for our bodies, and without poetry we cannot make use of all the material of life which we have accumulated by the exercise of reason. ' The body has then become too unwieldy for that which animates it.'   If Shelley's words are applicable to-day, poetry appears more than ever the natural ally of religion.   In our contemporary poetry, with all its imperfection of form and general dislike of sustained thinking, there is a remarkably clear conception that the poet's vocation is not merely to adorn life, but that he really helps to create it.   He ' redeems from decay the visitations of the divinity in man ' by keeping our imagination alive to the creative activity at work in the world of men—

The skill that must go forward and shape the world.

The poet's function is not to teach or to preach.   Imagination means enlargement of soul, and the poet's aim is the quest for beauty. Beauty is nothing in the world without the expression of it. The poet expresses it in words, the sculptor in stone, the smith in iron. Each has gained a victory over lifeless matter. Poems are not mere ' imitations ' of dreams. It is the process of transferring the dream into the outward reality of poetic form which involves labour and cost. The effort may be even more valuable than the work that is actually produced.[10] At this point, however, the modern conception of poetry as creative effort would part company with Shelley's curiously inconsistent statement that ' the mind in creation is as a fading coal, which some invisible influence, like an inconstant wind, awakens to transitory brightness. . . . When composition begins, inspiration is already on the decline.' The divine *afflatus* does not thus desert the poet in his effort at expression ; during that process it is never more truly present, as it continues to be present in the appreciation of the reader. The idea of poetry as creative effort is a modern development of Matthew Arnold's definition of poetry as the application of ideas to life, if not also an attempt at a modern and substitute rendering of the idea of the Divine Incarnation in humanity.

Poetry is indeed a spirit, which breathes when and where it wills. It is like a divine air which penetrates through the chinks of accepted and' traditional creeds, both moral and religious. Poetry suffers wrong when we seek to enthral it in the service of philosophy or of religion. Poetry speaks in the name of a spirit which it may consciously describe as Beauty, or Life, or God. The modern poet is apt to speak much more vaguely than his predecessors, and is often too easily satisfied to be a vehicle of the poetic impulse, without caring much or pausing long enough to understand the philosophy of the Life that animates his being. He is not so deeply concerned as the Victorian poets to enable us to view the world as a rational whole. He has the zest for the dramatic deep in his soul, and so long as life is preserved from torpor and something is being made or done, he does not sufficiently trouble himself to pass any moral, aesthetic, or philosophical judgment on the action involved. The worth of the drama tends to be measured by the fulness of life exhibited in it.

At the same time, consciously or unconsciously, the ' tough-minded ' view of life dominates the thinking of modern poetry. Especially regarding the facts of human suffering and their relation to a doctrine of Providence, the modern poetic view is a call to revise our conventional conceptions of the meaning of pain. Human pain has a deeper redemptive significance than the older philosophy allowed, and the question of redemption is no longer a subject which in philosophy is *taboo*, and suitable only for religious discussion. Browning may be looked upon as enshrining in his poetry the older religious point of view from which suffering was regarded, and his thought on this aspect of life is to-day not even obsolescent. It needs, however, to be extended. In the presence of the awfulness and shock of some of the pains and sorrows of human life, the advice—

> Learn, nor account the pang ; dare, never grudge
>   the throe,

seems hardly to do justice either to the dignity or courage of humanity in face of ' pangs ' and ' throes,' or to the devastating experiences of grief and loneliness they impose. There are some minds that would rest more calmly in Mr. Hardy's suggestion of a blind unconscious destiny at the heart of things, than in a God who uses such massive and terrifying tools in order to shape one puny human life toward perfection. If man be indeed, in Meredith's phrase, ' Earth's greatest venture,' he demands some other outlook than that to which a being is doomed, around whom all the great happenings of life, the vast universe of concrete facts with all their cruelty and bewilderment, revolve. Even Meredith's interpretation of them as ' thwackings ' of Nature, and his determination to take the discipline stoically, is altogether too unexpressive an attitude. Galileo, according to the legend, concluded his recantation of the Copernican position with the words, uttered *sotto voce*, ' Nevertheless, it does move.' The story may be taken as a symbol of the modern insistence in religion and philosophy on the creative influence of the individual life on a universe that is still in the process of making. The meaning of suffering is not anthropocentric. The individual life does *move* ; it does set in motion forces that are necessary to the shaping of the universe. All suffering has a redemptive significance. Modern tragedy, unlike the ancient, shows Man magnificent not in his defeat by, but in his superiority to the evil and hostile forces in Nature. Man is ' lord of his event.' The doctrine may be stated in an extreme form as by W. E. Henley in *Unconquerable*. Man may be represented as ' the captain of his soul,' an obvious and defiant exaggeration, which we nevertheless greet with the reverence due to it, because it is the voice of sincere passion and comes from one who passed his life as a hopeless cripple.

The poet does not inhabit a world of pure argument, but a world of passion and emotion. His business is not to make a new world, as has been said, but to advocate it ; not to save men's souls, but to make them worth saving. He makes men worth saving by keeping alive those human emotions and passions which are to-day the sign of a life that is striving not to escape from, or to submit to, but to conquer the misery, ugliness, and sin that stand in the way of a perfect world. Poetry is essential to the creation of a new world ; it reinvigorates and encourages the soul. Religious dogma must again become poetry, ' truth carried alive into the heart by passion ' in Wordsworth's phrase, if the world is to be changed. All dogmas were originally doxologies, and all creeds must be capable of being sung. ' Art alone,' says Sir Henry Newbolt, ' preserves the passions by transmuting them.' It transmutes them into the universal expression of poetry, universal because it appeals to the ' everyman ' in each of us.

Poetry, indeed, ' redeems from decay the visitations of the divinity in man.'

IV

The question may be asked whether the preference for shorter lyric poetry to-day makes it difficult to expect from our modern poets any really coherent philosophy of life.   William James has described as the ' pluralistic ' view of the universe his conception of life as ' an unfinished fight,' in which each individual, thinker, artist, poet, or worker does his creative part in advancing the good of a rational whole, as yet unrevealed. This does not exclude the idea of God, but He is only one individual among other individuals, although he may be *primus inter pares*. The ultimate result may not be complete success in the conquest of ugliness, misery, and evil, but only a betterment, described by the barbarous word ' meliorism.'   It is comparatively easy to criticise such a position from a philosophical point of view, and from a religious standpoint. This ' pluralism ' cannot be called a universe at all, and it certainly does not satisfy religious experience.[11]

Have we in the prevalence of the short lyric in modern poetry, which contains the presentation of isolated impressions of life—mostly everyday life—and is produced by the swift, intuitive vision of momentary experiences and passions, a mere reiteration in poetry of this pluralistic conception of life ?

If this pluralistic conception of life is only reiterated and given permanent form in poetry, we are moved to ask certain questions.   Why does William James's philosophy, with its conception of life doomed to incompleteness, and carrying with it no absolute assurance of the victory

of good over evil, and beauty over ugliness, leave us with a loud call to heroism
indeed, but with a haunting sense that
life may not after all succeed ?   Why does
a play of Mr. Bernard Shaw's, actuated
through and through by the same theory,
but teaching that poverty is a crime, that
romance is the real enemy, that life can
only yield its secret to a superman en-
dowed with a pitiless and unromantic
brain, leave us, wondering at the sword-
play of wit, but uninspired and chilled to
the bone ?   Why, on the other hand, do
the best modern lyrics, resting practically
on the same philosophy of life, and seizing
upon some fragment of the concrete
material of human experience, convey to
our hearts a sense of beauty and harmony
which is in itself a token of victory over
unwilling matter ?   Is not the reason of
the difference this, that it comforts and
strengthens us to see in the work of the

poet, as distinct from the philosopher, or the philosopher turned dramatist, a mind that has laid argument aside, and beholds the perplexing or painful experience, in an attitude of intuition, and that is strong enough in its detachment to do so ?   And the poet's intuition enables us also to see what was formerly unseen. Our lyric poetry tends to give us, even if but as a faintly-heard harmony, a suggestion of life as a rational whole, to which the philosopher has not yet attained.   In this argumentative and calculating age of ours, many of these poets in their short pieces, whose subjects are but broken fragments and isolated scenes of everyday existence, have suddenly, by their treatment of these, made us aware, however dimly, of another and imperishable world, much as Tennyson does in his ' flower in the crannied wall.' The part is seen to contain the secret of the whole, and the poet is capable of showing us that not merely ' in the meanest flower that blows,' but in the commonest sights and experiences of life there ' lurks an atmosphere of infinite suggestion.' Take Mr. Bridges' glorious love-lyric *I will not let thee go*, with its haunting suggestion of love's immortality :—

> I will not let thee go.
> I hold thee by too many bands :
>   Thou sayest farewell, and lo !
>   I have thee by the hands,
>   And will not let thee go ;

or Mr. Gordon Bottomley's *To Iron-founders and Others*,[12] which opens with a picture taken from a country whose natural aspect is slain by the fumes of furnaces. The power of man has ' brought down the firmament ' like a black pall. Man's vision may be ' machines for making more machines ' and he can change the whole face of Nature :—

The grass, forerunner of life, has gone ;
But plants that spring in ruins and shards
Attend until your dream is done ;
I have seen hemlock in your yards.

There is the conviction that the hidden powers of Nature thus blackened and defied are again slowly preparing themselves for conquest, and humanity will be led to nobler ' fashionings.'

The generations of the worm
Know not your loads piled on their soil ;
Their knotted ganglions shall wax firm
Till your strong flagstones heave and toil.

The cult of the lyric in our day is largely due to a reaction from a certain width and literalness of interpretation given by poets like Browning and Tennyson to some such principle as Wordsworth expressed when he said that ' Poetry is the impassioned expression on the face of science.' Wordsworth, clearly, never meant his words to mean that a poet must also be a scientist.

Wordsworth's perception of his subjects is not based on scientific but on mystical insight. He speaks of the celandine, not as a botanist, but as a mystic might :—

> Little flower !—I 'll make a stir,
> Like a great astronomer.

The poem gives no recognisable description of the celandine. When he speaks of the robin chasing a butterfly, he does not see a bird seeking his natural food, but a sight that mars the beauty and harmony of Nature :—

> If thou wouldst be happy in thy nest,
> O pious Bird ! whom man loves best,
> Love him or leave him alone.

'Leave him alone,' which every scientist knows the robin cannot do !.

Browning and Tennyson, on the other hand, in their attitude towards Nature, evidently work with a background of scientific knowledge, which is used to provide poetic material and suggestion. In Browning especially, we are made to feel that he has deeply studied the psychology of painting and sculpture. *The Grammarian's Funeral* shows that he understands to the depths the mind of the scholar. No fault need be found with this, and it is no unfounded charge that is levelled against contemporary poetry that we so often miss in it that background of culture and scholarship which the great Victorians possessed. There is to-day even a tendency to depreciate scientific knowledge as a necessary part of the poet's equipment. Mr. Drinkwater in *A Prayer* says :—

> We would not break the bars
> Thy wisdom sets about us ; we shall climb
> Unfettered to the secrets of the stars
> In Thy good time.

In *The Fires of God*,[13] which seems to have

a certain autobiographical interest, the writer speaks of an intellectual, a sort of 'Paracelsus aspires' stage in his spiritual development which he now deprecates as having cut him off from

> The holy sweet communion of men.

He was tempted to think of his fellows as those who

> Stumble darkly, unaware
> Of solemn mysteries
> Whereof the key is mine alone to bear.

The temptation, however, of the modern poet is not, as a rule, to intellectual exclusiveness. It is rather a temptation to forfeit the power of sustained thinking, to imagine that he who runs may best read, and to become so deeply involved in the very life he is describing that he is unable to find time for contemplation and reflection. *The Fires of God* is a significant and valuable description of a very general poetic attitude to-day in religion and philosophy.

The shorter lyric of to-day, however, does not necessarily mean that the poet has ceased to take a large view of life, or that our age has lost its capacity for the longer poem. Mr. Alfred Noyes's *Torch-Bearers* is an indication that poetry is again awakening to the romance of science, and that the long poem may be restored to its place in our literature. Even in the short lyric the poet may lead us far beyond his immediate subject, and suggest the boundless or may enable us to hear the secret music of the world. This is the effect of such short poems as Mr. Madox Hueffer's *The Portrait* or Mr. Siegfried Sassoon's *Everyone Sang*. The real poetic achievement, whether the poem be long or short, occurs when we are made to feel that a larger spiritual world seeks admission

at one of the many doors of this our
world of everyday. The poet's conscious
quest may be for beauty alone, but beauty
being a portion of the kingdom of God, is
alike to it in this also—when it is sought
and found, all other things are added.
Beauty signalises the presence of a certain
kind of life which is unlike any other kind,
inasmuch as it unifies and does not disin-
tegrate the external world or the world of
men. Intellectual activity is a form of
life that analyses and dissects : commercial
life both unifies men's interests and also
divides them sharply. In the acorn there
is a kind of life that becomes an oak with
sheltering branches and not a blade of
grass. In poetry there is a kind of life
that effects the kinship of all men. A
linnet's song heard amid the darkest
surroundings, singing on ' a blackened
bough in Hell,' enables men to communicate with one another, as in J. E.

Flecker's remarkable lyric, *Tenebris Inter-lucentem* :—

> A linnet who had lost her way
>   Sang on a blackened bough in Hell,
>   Till all the ghosts remembered well
> The trees, the wind, the golden day.
>
> At last they knew that they had died
>   When they heard music in that land,
>   And some one there stole forth a hand
> To draw a brother to his side.

The worship of Beauty will never lead to sectarian strife, unlike the cult of philosophy and dogmatic religion. The value of beauty is not diminished but increased by being shared. Therein lies the significance of the poetic revival to-day, and the contribution it is making to the interpretation of life.

> You are the link which binds us each to each,
> Passion, or too much thought, alone can end
> Beauty, the ghost, the spirit's common speech.[14]

THE POET AS CREATOR

Man,—as befits the made, the inferior thing,—

.   .   .   .   .   .

Repeats God's priocess in man's due degree,
Attaining man's proportionate result,—
Creates, no, but resuscitates, perhaps.

> ROBERT BROWNING, *The Ring and the Book.*

Thought which is only thought, the work of art which is only conceived, the poem which is no more than a dream, as yet cost nothing in toil; it is the material realisation of the poem in words, of the artistic conception in statue or picture, which demands effort.

> HENRI BERGSON, *Life and Consciousness.*

THE modern view of the evolution of life as a process of continual creation has its effect on the theory of the poet's art. The issue is raised in the quotation from Browning with which the chapter opens. Does the poet really create something new,

84

or does he merely resuscitate, give new life to what might otherwise perish ? If the world is in process of being built, it is contended that the philosopher, the statesman, the worker in wood and stone —like the poet—are each engaged in a creative process. The moralist and the saint are alike engaged in keeping alive and in adding to those forces of goodness and love, which inspire, direct, and cleanse the hearts of men in their creative work of building up ' a new Jerusalem.' Is the poet to be given only a single place in the long list of vocations ? His peculiar faculty is the imagination, and in a sense the poet, by keeping imaginative thinking alive in the form of poetry, is contributing to the success and efficiency of all the other vocations. The use of the imagination is not confined to poetry, but in his employment of language the poet identifies himself with and is an instrument of that

rhythmic movement which by poetic faith
—' that willing suspension of disbelief for
the moment ' as Coleridge calls it [1]—we
believe is at the heart of things. This
rhythmic movement is the core of the
poetic emotion.

The poetic ' emotion,' as Mr. Drinkwater
points out, must not be regarded as a
general synonym for what we commonly
call the ' emotions,' such as happiness and
despair, love and hate.[2] These are only
a portion of the material with which
poetry works. Probably Wordsworth has
this distinction in mind in his famous
Preface, when he alludes to poetry as
exhibiting ' the manner in which we
associate ideas in a state of *excitement*.'
The ' excitement ' may accompany a sensation, a perception, or an emotion. Where
it does appear, it fosters in the mind a
moment of intuition which brings us into
immediate touch with the hidden rhythmic

movement of things. An intellectual truth, a deed of sacrifice or daring, a sunset sky, a flower, a character of moral grandeur, originates that poetic intuition which may lie ' too deep for tears,' and may express itself in an impressive calm or a sublime faith. Poetry, in the sense of the poetic intuition or the poetic ' emotion, has right to more than a place in the list along with philosophy and craftsmanship. This poetic or creative emotion must govern and animate all successful search for truth, and every attempt at outward expression of ideas, no matter what the form of expression may be. Poetry is the most perfect expression of that internal rhythm of all Being. It is a divine energy, and draws its supplies from the source which supplies everything. By the loss of that imagination which is the soul of Poetry —that kind of visual thinking which is inseparable from real religious experience—

living religion becomes hardened into dogma ; lack of imagination is also responsible for much of the cruelty that is in the world and the satisfaction with things as they are. For want of imagination also, philosophy becomes mere dialectic, or the cult of a featureless Absolute. Blake is credited with the saying that lack of imagination is the sin against the Holy Ghost.

Wordsworth suggested that metre and rhyme are the outward forms of poetry ; that they are intended to restrain passion, and to make painful subjects endurable. Rhyme, however, is not essential to poetry, although it may be one form of musical expression. Rhythm, on the other hand, is of its essence. Rhythm is not a quality which the poet gives to an experienced emotion ; it is a quality which is given to him in the intuition itself. It is not his servant, but his master. Poetic emotion is always rhythmical. Metre does not restrain passion, but is one of its methods of utterance. The beats that fall in the verse have a regularity which belongs to all the secret powers of the universe. There is a rhythm in the movement of the tides and the courses of the stars. The coursing blood in our veins, the sap in the trees, the waves of light and sound are all rhythmic. The poetic faith is that in things spiritual, as in things material, there is a rhythmic order, a harmony and a beauty.[3] To experience and to utter this rhythm is to be in touch with ultimate truth.

I

The great bulk of our modern poetry deals with the life of action, the outward action of men. The work of Mr. Masefield is the most conspicuous example. It is also significant that the drama is becoming increasingly popular. We have, however, our cloistral and mystical poets, of whom perhaps the best known is Mr. de la Mare. Mr. Ralph Hodgson is one of the most restrained of our modern poets, who has exercised his restraint unfortunately on his output as well. He possesses a remarkable power of visualising ideas, and his poetry exhibits a mood of composure which may conceal from an unobservant reader the depth of reflective insight that lies hidden beneath. In the apparently whimsical representation of Time,[4] in the poem of that name, as ' an old gypsy-man ' ceaselessly driving his caravan from end to end of the world, instead of as the ancient figure with the scythe and the hour-glass, he has crystallised for us Bergson's thought of Time as a stream against which we cannot go, and of existence as a perpetual change. It is a poetical rendering of Heraclitus' saying that we cannot step into the same river twice.

> Last week in Babylon,
> Last night in Rome,
> Morning, and in the crush
> Under Paul's dome ;
> Under Paul's dial
> You tighten your rein—
> Only a moment,
> And off once again ;
> Off to some city
> Now blind in the womb,
> Off to another
> Ere that 's in the tomb.

Mr. Hodgson sometimes gives the outward impression that he does not seek to probe into the mystery of things. If, however, we read the short cameo-like poem, *The Mystery*, and remember that he wrote also *The Bull* and *The Song of Honour*, the judgment is suggested that the spiritual rest and intellectual calm of *The Mystery* has been won by the poet in the centre of the storm. In *The Song of Honour* he says that he hears the song of fighters

> At odds with fortune night and day,
> Crammed up in cities grim and grey
> As thick as bees in hives ;
> Hosannas of a lowly throng
> Who sing unconscious of their song,
> Whose lips are in their lives.

He hears this song of ' high heroic things,' and it blends with the whole ' harmonious hymn of being ' at an altar set up in his innermost soul :—

> I heard it all, I heard the whole
> Harmonious hymn of being roll
> Up through the chapel of my soul
> And at the altar die,
> And at the awful quiet then
> Myself I heard, Amen, Amen,
> Amen I heard me cry !

The Mystery is the fruit of a vision received in that ' awful quiet.'

He came and took me by the hand
  Up to a red rose tree,
He kept His meaning to Himself
  But gave a rose to me.

I did not pray Him to lay bare
  The mystery to me,
Enough the rose was Heaven to smell,
  And His own face to see.

II

The reproach is often levelled against our contemporary poetry that it lacks technical perfection. We are reminded of Andrea del Sarto, ' the faultless painter,' who, looking at a Rafael portrait complains that an arm is out of drawing, and attempts to put it right.

Give the chalk here—quick, thus the line should go!
Ay! but the soul! he's Rafael! rub it out!

It is impossible to imprison the ' soul ' of the painter in mere rules of technique.

     A man's reach should exceed his grasp,
Or what's heaven for! All is silver-grey
Placid and perfect with my art : the worse!

By ' soul ' Browning means experience. The first thing in a work of art is not technical perfection, but experience. The artist must begin with his own experience or with his imaginative and sympathetic appropriation of other men's experience. ' Soul ' is more than technique.

A similar line of thought seems to be present in T. E. Brown's *Opifex*.[5]   The poet, under the guise of a sculptor ' carving images from clouds,' is seen at work. Clouds are the most changeful and elusive of all subjects, and may be taken as standing for the changeful and elusive experiences of human life.   He is using colours which he, and he alone, can see, ' pressed from the pulp of dreams.'   The voice of an ' iconoclast ' is heard saying :—

Forbear !   Thou hast no tools wherewith to essay
The delicate waves of that elusive grain :
Wouldst have due recompense of vulgar pain ?
The potter's wheel for thee, and some coarse clay !

Apparently the 'iconoclast' is one who believes that art is chiefly a matter of technique, and of certain rules and traditions. 'Your skill,' he says, 'is very ordinary. You have not been properly taught! You do not know the Master, and all the Guild's secrets! You are outside the guild!'

> Thereat I rose, and from his presence passed,
>   But going, murmured :—' To the God above,
>   Who holds my heart, and knows its store of love,
> I turn from thee, thou proud iconoclast.'

God reveals to the poet that his work is accepted here and now, as part of the divine creative plan. It has been done out of 'the store of love '—that sympathetic and living touch with fleeting reality—wherewith the poet has viewed his subject.

Then on the shore God stooped to me, and said :—
>   ' He spake the truth : even so the springs are set
>   That move thy life, nor will they suffer let,
> Nor change their scope ; else, living, thou wert dead.

' This is thy life : indulge its natural flow,
   And carve these forms.   They may yet find a place
   On shelves for them reserved.   In any case,
I bid thee carve them, knowing what I know.'

III

The poet is a creator.   He gives us what
no one else has seen, at least as he has
seen it ;   what he alone was created in
order to create.   He has actually given
life to a new thing.   He has fathomed the
secret of that unknown, which is a portion
of everything.   ' Poetry,' says Professor
Mackail, ' which is a function of life, is
(like life) in constant flux or progress.   It
touches now one point of the whole, now
another.   That which it touches becomes
a real thing ;   and not only so, but it
becomes there and then the centre and
essence of reality.' [6]

The true poet knows that without experience no creative work is possible. That

experience is the channel of a passion and a life, ' whose fountains are within.'

> O Lady ! we receive but what we give,
> And in our life alone does nature live :
> Ours is her wedding-garment, ours her shroud ! [7]

It would be true to say that the poet makes an actual addition to reality. He actually increases the amount of life in the world, by the production of forms in which it can express itself. When one soul has succeeded in communicating with another — an achievement of all great poetry — we have life more abundantly. We pass, as in the moral sphere, from death to life when we love the brethren. The length of the poem does not really matter. Some short lyrics contain within them the secret of the universe, and there are

> jewels five-words long
> That on the stretched fore-finger of all time sparkle
>   for ever.

This power of 'making an addition to reality' is one that belongs to another and more familiar region of life. It perhaps explains why there is no child like my child, and no love like my love. This is not an amiable foolishness of love. I am able so to re-create the individuality of another by love, that beside it all else in the world pales, and my creation is 'all the world to me.'

> . . . A woman takes a mate,
> And like the patient builder governs him
> Into the goodman known through a countryside,
> Or the wise friend that the neighbours will seek out,
> And he, for all his love, may never know
> How she has nourished the dear fine mastery
> That bids him daily down the busy road
> And leaves her by the hearth.[8]

IV

How shall we define the material on

which the poet exercises his creative power ?
Is it language alone ?

> The statue, Buonarotti said, doth wait
> Thralled in the block, for me to emancipate ;
> The poem, saith the poet, wanders free
> Till I betray it to captivity.

What corresponds to the block and what
to the statue in poetic activity ? Is language the whole material with which the
poet must work in order to embody his
ideas, corresponding to the marble of the
sculptor, or the pigments and canvas of
the painter ? Shelley regards the poet's
vehicle of expression in language as superior
to stone or pigment. The marble offers a
certain physical resistance to the sculptor's
chisel, which ' interposes between conception and expression ' ; language, on the
other hand, ' is a more direct representation of the actions and passions of our
internal being.' He means that language

is a product of the imagination, of thought alone, and therefore contains within itself that which is naturally responsive to the attack of the poet's imagination. This is hardly true to the experience of any one —not to speak of poets—who is fated to employ words as his particular vehicle of expression. We know the joy of the moment when the right word is found. Do we not know also the moments when language ' offers a determined resistance to thought,' when words will not appear at the appropriate moment and of the appropriate kind, nor array themselves, as Coleridge said they must, both in prose and in poetry, ' in the best order.' Language on its physical side, as collections of letters and sounds, is an obstacle too often felt to be not only disobedient but impervious to the influence of imagination. Poetry, as Shelley well knew, is more than decorative word-painting, and, really, no words are used in the same sense twice. Moreover, words may ' half-conceal and half-reveal the thought within,' and it is undoubtedly true that they are, in themselves, quite inadequate to utter the experience even of the most consummate artist. The effect of all great poetry is in the end not to speak, but to suggest the truth ; and this power of suggestion indicates that the heart of poetry lies much deeper than even ' the best words in the best order.' The material with which the poet works, as we shall see later, is much more than language.

On the other hand, the very outward medium which the artist employs, while it is in one sense an obstacle, is in another and most significant sense a powerful ally. It is chosen because the perception which the artist has, demands just this kind of material for its particular expression ; in the very process of expression, in words, in stone, in paint, or in the musical tone, the artist is conscious that the very material is coming to his aid. Compare the thought in Mr. John Freeman's *Music Comes* :—

> Music comes
> Strangely to the brain asleep !
> And I heard
> Soft, wizard fingers sweep
> Music from the trembling string,
> And through remembering reeds
> Ancient airs and murmurs creep ;
> Oboe, oboe following,
> Flute calling clear high flute,
> Voices faint, falling mute,
> And low jarring drums.[9]

Browning, who knows so accurately the internal struggles and hindrances of the artist, has thus imaginatively described those supreme moments in the greatest artistic expression when the work is done with a perfect ease, and even the external

material seems to yield itself willingly to
thought and touch :—

>   Marble !—'neath my tools
> More pliable than jelly—as it were
> Some clear primordial creature dug from depths
> In the earth's heart, where itself breeds itself,
> And whence all baser substance may be worked ;
>
>   .   .   .   .
>
> Refine it off to air, you may—condense it
> Down to the diamond ;—it is not metal there,
> When o'er the sudden speck my chisel trips ?
> —Not flesh, as flake off flake I scale, approach,
> Lay bare those bluish veins of blood asleep ?
> Lurks flame in no strange windings where, surprised
> By the swift implement sent home at once,
> Flushes and glowings radiate and hover
> About its track ? [10]

Similarly every painter knows the direction and control that is exercised upon his
activity according as his work is done on
fresco or on canvas, in water-colour or in
oil. The musician knows that there is one
voice of the flute, another of the cornet,

another of the violin. Similarly the poet feels that the materials he works with are not unresponsive forms. Words, too, are more than sounds ; they are garners stored with history and the experience of generations of their users. Languages, also, have their distinctive characters, and forms of expression and metre suited to one language do violence to another. Even words seem to welcome the emotion, the rhythm which the poet brings, and respond to his touch. This joyous welcome is the sign of creation. It is poetry.

The material of the poet, however, is composed of much more than words. Set the same words in another order and in other emphases, and you will have at the best inferior prose. The language of a perfect poem is no doubt inviolably wedded to the material of the poem, but it is only a part of that material. It ought not to be possible to render the same poetic moment in other words, but only in these words, in that particular order, and in no other. There is something inevitable in all true poetry, a prophetic element, a sense of 'thus saith the Lord,' which demands a deeper and greater source than the poet's individual and isolated imagination. The material has encountered his imagination, and has not been produced by it. It is, again, a visitation of divinity in outward form which the poet as a kind of sacred duty preserves from decay. Poetic energy blossoms on the lips of the poet, as the moral and religious power of the prophet is concentrated on his lips, his immediate point of contact with his audience. ' Woe is me, for I am a man of unclean lips ' is much more than a confession of verbal error. ' Poetry is the blossom and the fragrancy of all human knowledge, human thoughts, human passions, emotions, language.' [11] Words are but the immediate point of contact of the poet with the soul of his readers.

The block of marble lies at Michelangelo's door. In the heart of it, the *Pieta* or the *David* is awaiting Michelangelo to set it free. Nevertheless, the material with which he works, malleable to his hand, is not only marble, but includes his own overmastering passionate and intuitive desire. Do not let us say that an artist, a poet, or a sculptor has ideals. Ideals may cost nothing or they may be only the frozen remains of desires that once were alive. The artist has desires or ' values,' not ideals. Values carry within themselves a force that presses on to their realisation ; they are like the sun, which not only gives light, but also the warmth and energy by which all things live. To recall Bergson's words again, it is the writing of the poem, the painting of the picture, which costs, and the effort is more precious even than the work it produces. This effort also is included in Michelangelo's material. Moreover, the material includes also his search for just this block and no other, his selection of it, his rejection of this and that ; the opposition, indifference, or favour of popes and patrons ; the chances and fortunes (in his case) of contemporary wars ; the crass hindering conceptions of art in his own day ; every condition that stands in the way of the full flow of artistic expression. All these go to form his material, his matter, at one time reluctant, at another a willing instrument, at another a passionate stimulus. In the end his statue is an addition to reality. He has produced what had never been in the world before and can never be mechanically repeated.

Similarly, a poem represents a victory over all that hinders, curbs, and thwarts the free expression of a passion for Beauty.

Ugly or tragic, heroic or beautiful, kindly or cruel, the actual point may be, at which the poet's perception touches reality ; it may even seem a freak of accident, or a sport of fate. The poet seeks to set it in its place, as an integral part of the whole of life ; as something otherwise meaningless, like a musical note apart from the tune.

It may, however, be suggested that there are still some materials inherently unsuitable for poetry, and offering in the nature of things determined resistance to the creative effort of the poet. One is inclined to agree with a critic [12] who sees in such creations as Mr. Gordon Bottomley's Regan in *King Lear's Wife*,—chosen apparently only because they have a peculiar ' energy '—' a Pyrrhic victory over reluctant matter.' [13]   Many more victories like these and poetry is lost !   All the subjects rejected as pariahs by previous poetry can never hope to be admitted to the caste. No matter what the theme suggested, the poet of to-day has an overwhelming and often an overweening confidence in his own powers of creation. He forgets that

Man's breath were vain to light a virgin wick ;—
Half-burned out, all but quite quenched wicks o'
    the lamp
Stationed for temple-service on this earth,
These indeed let him breathe on and relume.[13]

GOOD AND EVIL IN POETRY.   CAN THE DEVIL WRITE POETRY ?

The devil can do many things. But the devil cannot write poetry. He may mar a poet, but he cannot make a poet. Among all the temptations wherewith he tempted St. Anthony, though we have often seen it stated that he howled, we have never seen it stated that he sang.

FRANCIS THOMPSON, *Shelley*.

Good and Evil we know in the field of this World grow up together almost inseparable. . . . Those confused seeds which were imposed on *Psyche* as an incessant labour to cull out, and sort asunder, were not more intermixt.

JOHN MILTON, *Areopagitica*.

MR. BERNARD SHAW, with a ruthlessness that outbids Plato, banishes poets as well as philosophers and ' founders of religion ' from his ideal state.   Romance, in his eyes, is a moral danger, and he has given fresh

currency to the slander that imagination
—poetic, religious, or speculative—is the
chief faculty by which we tell lies.

> And don't you deal in poetry, make-believe,
> And the white lies it sounds like ?

The hope of the world lies in the coming of
a race of supermen who understand and
therefore control the forces of life, 'instead
of blindly stumbling hither and thither in
the line of least resistance,' by which I
suppose he means, among others, the line
opened up by the romantic imagination.
Logic and argument alone can save the
world, and he would subscribe to Hesiod's
saying that Virtue, Heaven has ordained,
shall be reached by the sweat of the fore-
head.   Moral and spiritual iconoclasm like
Mr. Shaw's needs no poetry. Iconoclasm
is the most prosaic, as the most socially
disintegrating of all vocations ; for reason,
without the poetic imagination, is ever

disruptive and anti - social. To recall Flecker's striking visualisation in *Tenebris Interlucentem*, poetry is a song in darkness. Poetry, when it deals with the darker side of life, fosters a mood in which those whose lives are shadowed by affliction and wrong recognise the faces and reach out for the sympathies of their fellows. Poetry's influence, like religion's, is a social influence, binding society more closely together.

The purpose of this chapter is to discuss that ever-recurring, very thorny, and dangerously commonplace question of the treatment of ugliness and evil in literature, more particularly in poetry. If the word were not seriously overworked, I would say that the discussion handles the question of the return to Realism in modern poetry. I assume, at the outset, that, in literature, —apart, of course, from purely scientific literature—the only permissible treatment of evil must always be ' poetic.' To bring order and harmony out of the disorder and discordance which are the distinguishing marks of ugliness, must always be an integral part of the writer's purpose. It is an act of violence to employ the dissecting table for human passions. A writer must not behave like a scientist, and masquerade as a poet or novelist. The action of the human soul cannot be analysed and measured like physical matter.[1] The poet deals with living men and women. How can he dare

Bid each conception stand while, trait by trait,
My hand transfers its lineaments to stone ?
Will my mere fancies live near you, their truth—
The live truth, passing and repassing me,
Sitting beside me ?[2]

The increasing popular interest to-day in psychology has had some baleful effects both on poetry and on the novel. Mr. Lascelles Abercrombie, for example, in his *Emblems of Love,* with all the essential nobility and power of his work, has forgotten that an incident like the peasant girl's falling in love with the rebel's severed head is not a stage in the growth of love. It is love, not on its way up but on its way down, and already pretty far down. The idea is decadent, and a mere repetition of the wearisome and repellent theme of Oscar Wilde's *Salome*.

I

Every sincere student of poetry to-day must feel the need of simple and elementary principles enabling him to decide two questions that specially confront him. These are : first, What is the difference between good and bad poetry in an artistic sense ? and second, What relation has poetry to the question of morals ? The answer to the first question does not here greatly concern us. It is difficult. chiefly because

the educated reader will always decide it
ultimately by instinct and by personal
preference. Moreover, the answer when
it is given would in all probability merely
state, in academic or scientific language,
what has already been decided instinctively and unconsciously. The first question is in the end a question of ' taste,' and
probably, as Sir Henry Newbolt has said,
' Every one gets the poetry he deserves.'
The second question is more pressing, and,
to most minds, really includes the first.
Most men find it impossible to enjoy
poetry, however perfect technically, which
revolts their enlightened moral judgment.
Unless, therefore, we are to separate the
question of form in poetry from the question of its substance—an unwarrantable
and impossible attitude in view of what
has been said about the extent of the
poet's material — the first question is
really answered in the reply given to the

second.   It is all the more necessary, therefore, that the poet should be protected
from any illicit interference with artistic
liberty by a prejudiced moral judgment.

A poet has not only to create his poem,
but, in a sense, he has also to create his
audience.   His audience may already have
this or that notion of what is beautiful and
therefore pleasant.   The aim of poetry is
to give pleasure, but this aim must not be
understood to mean that pleasure is communicated only when we are reminded of
what we have usually found to be pleasant.
For the poet to yield to the demand that
what is conventionally pleasant must alone
form his ' subject,' would be to abrogate
entirely his creative function, to be a
traitor to his art, and to fall to the level
of the mere entertainer.   Poetry, like religion, chooses the ugly only in order to
fashion it into a fairer form ; modern
poetry especially has an almost boundless,

and incurably adventurous faith that no
ugliness is invincible.

We may remind ourselves, at this stage,
of what has already been said of the return
in modern poetry to the conception of
Beauty as a courageous achievement, as
against an invertebrate aestheticism.
Professor Bernard Bosanquet has drawn
a useful distinction between ' easy ' beauty
and ' difficult beauty.' [3] ' Easy' beauty is
that kind which ' is *prima facie* pleasant
practically to every one.' To say that it
is ' easy ' to appreciate the beauty of a
simple tune, or a rose, or the human form,
is not to depreciate that kind of beauty,
as though it were trivial and superficial.
There is, however, a ' difficult ' beauty,
the beauty say of *The Widow in the Bye-
Street* or of Shakespeare's Falstaff scenes.
It is a beauty that demands of the reader
concentration of thought, depth of sympathetic feeling, and absence of conventional

restraint ; in brief, an independence of judgment and detachment from prejudice which ought to be the fruit of education and training. The appreciation of ' difficult ' beauty means a culture not so much of mind as of imagination. It is a moral quality. It is that view of nature and of human life which may be described as the truth told or listened to, lovingly. Poetry is ' love talking musically.'

The chief hindrance to the appreciation of this ' difficult ' beauty, which represents a real victory over reluctant material, is that shrinking from what is evil, painful, or ugly which Aristotle long ago described when he spoke of ' the weakness of the spectator.' The spectator desires to spare himself ; perhaps it means also that he desires, on moral grounds, to spare his fellows ; to shield their gaze from a world which is too poignant in its sorrows and too defiant in its sins. Frequently it may

be a kind of selfish shrinking from evil,
a symptom of moral despair or moral
cowardice ; of dislike for moral discomfort,
or of a shallow optimism that would cloak
the existence in real life of such piercing
tragedy. Beauty, it is said, demands the
happy ending to the story, and the spec-
tacle of ' beauty overthrown ' may seem
an immoral conclusion.

> They who are sceptred of the poet's race
>   Their high dominion bear by this alone—
>   That they report the world as they have known
> The world, nor seek with slavish hands to trace
> Poor profitable smiles upon the face
>   Of truth when smiles are none, nor fear to own
>   The bitterness of beauty overthrown,
> But hold in hate the gilded lie's disgrace.[4]

Every one can recognise this ' weakness
of the spectator.' It may be a serious
hindrance to the appreciation and growth
of art, and is a frequent cause of its

degradation. On the other hand, the artist must remember that he, too, may have his weakness. His defect may be that he so presents his subject as to challenge directly the weakness, and not the strength of the spectator ; to afford his readers little encouragement to overcome their shrinking and to enter upon what must often be in this world a courageous and self-sacrificing quest for beauty. The artist may tend to forget that character must reinforce intellectual capacity in the appreciation of beauty, both in audience and in poet. He has the right to demand undoubtedly that his audience, if he is a poet, should be teachable : the audience, on the other hand, is justified in demanding certain qualities in the teacher. He must take a large view of his subject, and must give a picture of the whole of life as men live it. Dickens, for example, never errs in this direction, notwithstanding all his realistic pictures of crime and poverty. His poor people and his victims of evil are never wholly unhappy. Dickens by his insistence on the happiness of the unhappy was by no means unsuccessful as a reformer and he helped to dry many bitter tears. It is ultimately character which determines whether men shall be teachable ; and it is character that can alone give the poet a large and comprehensive view of his subject.

Mr. Thomas Hardy in *In Tenebris* speaks of himself as one

> Who holds that if way to the Better there be, it
>> Exacts a full look at the Worst,
> Who feels that delight is a delicate growth
>> Cramped by crookedness, custom, and fear.

In a recent comment on those lines [5] he tells us that the ' full look at the Worst ' is ' the exploration of Reality, and its frank recognition stage by stage along the

survey, with an eye to the best consumma-
tion possible.' 'Reality' is apparently
identical with 'the Worst,' and the only
possible ameliorating influence is 'lovingkindness operating through scientific knowledge.   The essential disability in Mr.
Hardy's outlook on life, as we know it, is
that he has never been able to take a large
enough view of human experience, so as to
include the verdict of those who have
found it glad and joyous, especially when
the joy—as the highest joy must ever be—
is one that in its own hard experience has
transmuted pain and suffering into a
strength and a glory.   Out of the slain
eater this experience has brought meat,
and men naturally dislike lingering by the
decaying corpse.   Mr. Hardy undoubtedly
artificially increases the odds against some
of his characters.   We miss in him that
quality which Matthew Arnold attributed
to Chaucer, 'his large, free, simple, clear

yet kindly view of human life.'   The most
teachable among ' spectators ' are not
those who have blithely solved the riddle
of this ' unintelligible world,' or have
accepted ready-made solutions ; but those
who have worn or, however feebly, attempt
to wear their suffering, as men might wear
a decoration.   ' Lovingkindness, operating
through scientific methods,' seems a con-
tradiction in terms.   Charity organisation
is a means and not an end.   Lovingkindness—of which Mr. Hardy has abund-
ance—must ever assume in the first place
that life is worth living ; otherwise it is
a mere pathetic futility, maimed at the
outset.   Scientific method, on the other
hand, would belie its title unless it left the
question of the worth of life to the moralist.
Mr. Hardy has much to say against breezy
and shallow optimism, but seems to have
forgotten that there are those whose
optimism is strongly and deeply founded

—very different persons from those described in the lines—

The stout upstanders chime, All 's well with us :
   ruers have nought to rue !
And what the potent so often say, can it fail to be
   somewhat true ?
Breezily go they, breezily come ; their dust smokes
   round their career,
Till I think I am one born out of due time, who has
   no calling here.[6]

Mr. Hardy regards his so-called pessimism as not worse than that which underlies the Christian idea, forgetful that the pessimism underlying the Christian faith is itself a product of faith in the Incarnation—leaving out of account the question whether Christian pessimism be justified or not. It does not arise from a ' full look at the Worst,' but from a full look at what men believe to be the best of which human nature and human life is capable.

Aristotle has a saying that whatever is

beautiful must not only be a perfect whole, but must possess a certain 'magnitude.' It must be presented on such a scale that the relation of the subject to the whole of life may be clearly perceived. There are individual poems of Mr. Hardy's which actually transgress this principle. The notorious case is the poem *Royal Sponsors*, which has aroused the opposition of many good literary critics, to whom Mr. Hardy replies in the Preface already mentioned. The poem describes the christening of a dead infant. The child is the son of a courtier, and on the morning of the cere-mony is found to have died. The King and Queen were to act as sponsors, and it is resolved to conceal what has happened and to go on with the ceremony, including the use of the Jordan water that has been provided. Why? The motive, if it is not pure love of an escapade, is simply that the servants may have their feast, and the

court its ball, arranged in honour of the
event. A painter knows that not all
nature is beautiful, and that his subject
needs certain lights and settings. Neither
is all life beautiful. Mr. Hardy's subject
is ugly, and it could only become beautiful
if it were caught in the light of Fate, or
Love, or Self-sacrifice, or Pity. Not a
trace of the working of any of these is
found in the poem. Mr. Hardy says that
the poem is ' a dramatic anecdote ' having
' a satirical or humorous intention.' To
most readers, however, the incident, intended to be humorous, seems to have no
point, and the defence cannot even be
raised that the poet has been able to do
what Professor Bosanquet calls that ' very
clever and difficult thing, to tell a story
whose point is that it has no point.' [7] The
incident in the poem has no ' magnitude.'
The motives that govern all the parties
concerned are not derived even from a

spirit of defiant hostility or deliberate flouting of religious conviction or ritual. A certain pathos might even have been present, and it is entirely absent. The subject is itself ugly, random, and freakish, and remains so after the poet has done with it.

I would not have dwelt so long on this particular poem did it not illustrate by its very defect certain nobler qualities that are found in the rest of Mr. Hardy's poetry. What makes his outlook on life bearable, and helps to win for his poetry the place it occupies in men's hearts to-day, in spite of its plaintiveness and despair, is its entire freedom from any cynical view of human nature. Egdon Heath in *The Return of the Native* is a mirror of ' man's nature— neither ghastly, hateful, nor ugly ; neither commonplace, unmeaning, nor tame ; but like man slighted and enduring.' No conception of human experience, however sombre and sorrowful, can be cynical which pictures the human soul in conflict with the gigantic forces of the universe. Mr. Hardy's appeal to men's hearts is really due to his general observance, both in his prose and in his poetry, of the ' magnitude ' of human suffering. Pain, sorrow, and human wrong-doing, presented as great in their piteous expostulation against the insensibility of the universe, are legitimate subjects of poetry. This ' magnitude ' is finely expressed in Mr. Hardy's *At a Lunar Eclipse* :—

> Thy shadow, Earth, from Pole to Central Sea,
> Now steals along upon the Moon's meek shine
> In even monochrome and curving line
> Of imperturbable serenity.
>
> How shall I link such sun-cast symmetry
> With the torn troubled form I know as thine,
> That profile, placid as a brow divine,
> With continents of moil and misery ?

And can immense Mortality but throw
So small a shade, and Heaven's high human scheme
Be hemmed within the coasts yon arc implies ?

Is such the stellar gauge of earthly show,
Nation at war with nation, brains that teem
Heroes, and women fairer than the skies ?

Mr. Hardy's men and women cry for succour, and there is none to help ; yet they seek redemption. This is a nobler conception of man than the self-sufficient one which represents him as shaping his own destiny, and accounts largely for Mr. Hardy's human appeal to his contemporaries.

The only justification for sincere and realistic treatment of ugliness and evil in literature is in order to display it in all its sheer defiant hostility to the central harmony of the universe. Sin must ever appear, as in Meredith's magnificent *Lucifer in Starlight*, in conflict with the ' army of unalterable law.' We must not demand of literature, as we may of religion, that it should resolve or remove the moral discord ; far less that it should gloss it over, or weave a veil of sentiment around it. Of Poetry, at least, we have a right to ask only that it should lift us up into that mood both of sympathy and of detachment—sympathetic because detached and for the moment uninvolved—in which we can judge of the real issues at stake. This mood of sympathetic detachment is itself a sign that the poet has been able to take up a stand outside the range of the forces that seem to overwhelm the human spirit. This cannot be an attitude of despair ; for despair is always silent. Mr. Hardy's world—especially in *The Dynasts*—horrible as its writhing often is, is yet on such a tragic scale that our pity and terror are not satisfied to have merely an ' outlet,' as Aristotle would have it ; we welcome the Chorus of Pities, which keeps alive the

redemptive instinct in human nature, and
calls for succour on the redemptive forces
of the universe. Burns realised the compassionate and imaginative function of poetry
in relation to morals when he wrote :—

> Wi' wind and tide fair i' your tail
> Right on ye scud your seaway ;
> But in the teeth o' baith to sail,
> It maks an unco leeway.[8]

The compassionate and imaginative
function of poetry is conspicuous in Mr.
Masefield's narrative poem, *The Everlasting
Mercy*. The poem came with a certain
shock to certain classes of readers to whom
its religious idea would make a powerful
appeal. The conception of religious experience which is preserved in the poem is
of extraordinary value, and the value would
have been greatly diminished without the
poet's realistic method of treatment. Notwithstanding, it is evident that there has
been at times inadequate selection of the

material at the poet's disposal ; for selection is also an important part of interpretation. The complaint is not that the material is coarse and horrible, but that the presentation is unnecessarily realistic. Owing to the excess of a boundless sincerity, Mr. Masefield has at moments increased the horror by calling attention to it, as a man might use immoderate gesticulation in speech. At times his material seems to have mastered him, and the product of his own art carries him away. He has, in a kind of humility, been blind to what his own imagination has succeeded in creating, and forgets that his art makes its own deep impression. Occasionally he leaves too little for the reader's imagination to do, and pays too little attention to what the imagination of the poet has already done.

These criticisms of Mr. Masefield's work have been made many times. They are

repeated here only in order that the ground
may be cleared to appreciate his success
in giving the proper ' magnitude ' to that
adventure of the soul which is his theme.
The poem is a sign, rivalled only by Francis
Thompson's *Hound of Heaven*, that in
modern poetry religious experience is again
coming to its own as a subject for poetry.
Mr. Masefield clearly did not choose his
own subject ; rather does it seem to have
been chosen for him. I do not mean that
Saul Kane is an actual historical character.
The longing seems to have entered the
poet's heart, like ' the bright bird ' in the
Dauber, to write a poem on the regenera-
tion of a blackguard. We have been
waiting for the interpretation of such a
subject by a real poet. Mr. Masefield is
not of those who simply know by report
stories of sordid passion ; the kind of
poet, as Professor Bradley says, ' who
strolls about the lanes or plods the London

streets with an umbrella for a sword, and who has probably never seen a violent deed in his life, or for a moment really longed to kill so much as a critic.' [9]   Mr. Masefield's power is due to the fact that, in his wanderings and adventures by sea and land, the violent actions and passions he depicts are actually like the things he saw and heard.   The theme of *The Everlasting Mercy* is the conversion of Saul Kane — poacher and libertine — and his choice of such a theme is one of the earliest signs in our modern poetry of a return to religious experience as an element in reality. Art has too long rejected religion—discouraged it may be by the exclusive claims of religion itself—as a portion of its experience, either because it had learned to fear religion as its natural enemy, or did not understand it.   The reproach is no longer deserved after such a work as *The Everlasting Mercy*, or the work of poets

like Mr. Gerald Gould and Mr. Robert
Graves. Mr. Masefield has given to one
kind of religious experience, the catas-
trophic, its proper magnitude. He has
presented in *The Everlasting Mercy* much
more than a vivid and conventionally interpreted example of religious conversion.
A certain Scottish minister was once
visiting a parishioner on his death-bed.
The man's life had been wild, and he was
telling to sympathetic ears the story of the
great deliverance that had come to him
through a religious experience. He then
added sharply, ' Doctor ! ye winna mak'
an anecdote o' me.' A similar plea needs
to be entered for the use of *The Everlasting
Mercy*. Saul Kane's conversion is much
more than a religious anecdote. Mr. Masefield has understood and interpreted his
subject. The subject may have come to
him amid the sights and sounds of Nature.
He has kept it there steadily all through

the poem. There is none of the hot and fever-laden atmosphere of the religious meeting. The God with whom Saul Kane is at enmity is the God of the great spaces and the open air. In *The Everlasting Mercy* Nature to the regenerate Saul Kane has taken on a ' moral ' meaning hitherto unseen. It is in the language of Nature that he describes the influence at work in his spirit. The healing touch that is laid upon him is like the cooling breeze :—

> I opened window wide and leaned
> Out of that pig-stye of the fiend
> And felt a cool wind go like grace
> About the sleeping market-place.

The coming of the deliverance is like the rhythmic power that moves the tide :—

> The water 's going out to sea,
> And there 's a great moon calling me ;
> But there 's a great sun calls the moon,
> And all God's bells will carol soon
> For joy and glory and delight
> Of some one coming home to-night.

Mr. Masefield has understood that the conflict of good and evil in the human heart is
a portion of the vaster conflict of elements
in the universe.   He has received from the
imagination of the greatest Poet of all, who
thus described the success of the feeble
ministry of his disciples on a scale that
must have filled them with wonder when
he said, ' When you were away, I beheld
Satan as lightning fall from heaven ' ; who
knew that such an experience of victory
has its reverberations in the furthest star—
' There is joy in the presence of the angels
of heaven over one sinner that repenteth.'
The fine lyric description of ' a new heaven
and a new earth ' in the imagination of a
man who at once felt the whole universe
against him, is one of the most striking
contributions in modern times to the
understanding of the New Testament.

II

Friction and antagonism may arise between art and morality. How far is an artist limited in his choice of subject ? Can we discover any principle which will commend itself to any sane mind as fitted to govern our thinking on this matter ? The conduct and interpretation of life must not be handed over either to the artist or to the moralist, in isolation from one another. Such an alternative means both bad art and bad morality.

I think we may still discover this guiding principle in the interpretation of poetry, of which we are in search, lurking in a sentence or two from Wordsworth's famous Preface. He allows his readers to suppose ' that by the act of writing in verse an author makes a formal engagement that he will gratify certain known habits of association : that he not only thus apprises the reader that certain classes of ideas and expressions will be found in his book, but that others will be carefully excluded.' These words contain much more than an apparent capitulation to the weaknesses and prejudices of the reader. Wordsworth, himself, has some apposite words to utter regarding the influence of traditional prejudice, and the application of pre-established codes of decision to the interpretation of poetry. ' While they are perusing this book,' he says, ' they should ask themselves if it contains a natural delineation of human passions, human characters, and human incidents ; and if the answer be favourable to the author's wishes, that they should consent to be pleased in spite of that most dreadful enemy to our pleasures, *our own pre-established codes of decision.*' Wordsworth would certainly not have been prepared for the lack of reserve in the choice of subjects which appears in modern poetry ; but that is due far less to any moral prejudice on his part than to his general theory of poetry, in accordance with which Man is subordinated to the fairer aspects of Nature.

We speak of unsuitable and unsavoury subjects. Our attention requires to be directed away from the adjectives to the noun. What is really meant by the poet's ' subject ' ? With these sentences from Wordsworth's Preface and Professor Bradley's lecture *Poetry for Poetry's Sake* as guides, we may make the attempt to define this very ambiguous word ' subject.' Wordsworth speaks of ' certain classes of ideas and expressions ' which will be excluded from his book. By these he must mean not merely words and phrases, nor brute facts, but interpretations, renderings of facts. They are not really facts in themselves to which readers apply ' codes of decision,' but the poet's interpretations of them. As readers or critics of poetry we are not so much concerned with the subject as with the poet's rendering of his subject. In a sense, that rendering *is* the subject. It is not the thing as it was before the poet touched it, but the thing as it is, after his creative touch has re-made it, which is in question and which we are required to judge. We must appreciate a poem, a story, or a picture, not by the subject as it is perceived by us who may not be artists or poets, but by the subject as seen by the artist and presented to our minds.

Let us take two familiar illustrations from the literature of the gospels. In the parable of the Prodigal, two renderings of the same subject are given us. There is the curt, brutal, and no doubt correct rendering of him who said, ' When this thy son came, which hath devoured thy living with harlots, thou killedst for him the fatted calf ' : the other is, ' This thy brother was dead, and is alive again ; and was lost, and is found.' The latter is a concise epitome of the whole ' subject,' containing all its pathos and passion, joy and tragedy. The one rendering we reject, the other we accept. Take another example. Our Lord's host on one occasion gave a rendering of a woman's broken life. ' This man, had he been a prophet, would have known what manner of woman this is that toucheth him.' The facts could not be gainsaid, but the guest, with a quiet decision, rejected the rendering, and gave instead his own, which it has since been the aim of his true followers in all ages to prefer. The first was the kind of rendering to be expected from a man who had made such a tactless blunder as to offer an entertainment to a heart already beginning to break. There is nothing more impressive anywhere in literature than the aesthetic fitness of appeal of the woman's tears and perfume, quite spontaneously and instinctively made, to the heart of Jesus, who in growing loneliness of soul had hitherto looked in vain for any such intelligent human recognition of the meaning and purpose of his pain. The two ' souls,' Jesus' and the woman's, had by poetic expression communicated with one another. The Pharisee can make nothing of such a subject. Indeed, his touch upon it is destructive, not creative. The Evangelists have given us a treatment of a moving human experience, seen through eyes other than their own. They have given us a new thing, an addition to reality, and what this woman did is preserved in the poetry of religion as a memorial for ever. The principle we employ in reading the gospels, or other scriptures with their realistic presentation of life, is precisely the same as we must employ in appreciating the subject of a work of art.

To lay this stress, as we are bound to do,

on the *treatment* of a subject, as distinct from
the subject itself—what Professor Bradley
calls the ' substance ' in an effort to remove
the ambiguity already mentioned—is also
to assume that the poet has something he
desires to communicate to his audience.
All art, as has been said, means that we
have something to communicate.   No poet
dare claim that he is independent of his
audience ; otherwise his action in writing,
printing, publishing is a sheer contradic-
tion.   He is justly resentful if ' pre-established codes of decision ' are used to hamper
the free expression of his art ; on the other
hand, while he resents the prejudices, he
must have sufficient trust in human nature
to respect the powers of decision and of
judgment which his readers possess.   He
has no doubt, as we have seen, often to
create the very discrimination and ' taste '
which ought to be directed on his work ;
but he must also remember that the very

powers which enable him to utter are essentially the same powers which enable his readers to enjoy his work in the fullest sense. Poetic power in the poet is in the end the same as poetic receptiveness in the reader. Both stand or fall together. The mind that is able to behold, even through another's eyes, a thing of beauty, creates the very image in which the perception is enclosed. Mr. Bridges, looking upon certain glorious examples of Greek art, sings :—

> Is all this glory, I said, another's praise ?
> Are these heroic triumphs things of old ;
> And do I dead upon the living gaze ?
> Or rather doth the mind, that can behold
> The wondrous beauty of the works and days,
> Create the image that her thoughts enfold ? [10]

Right appreciation of beauty is also a creative act. The poet makes his readers share in his creative effort, and bids them rejoice with him in the discovery of a beauty that has been obscured or lost.

Is artistic freedom possible if the artist must consider other minds ? The answer is that true freedom both in art and in morals demands a social sense, and involves a reference to other lives than our own.

One may do whate'er one likes
In Art ; the only thing is, to make sure
That one does like it—which takes pains to know.[11]

What one likes ? It ' takes pains to know ' for the artist must respect other minds. Conscience also must take ' pains to know ' ; we must be sure that our ' good will,' as Kant calls it, deserves to become a regulating principle for all men. It is with aesthetic ' liking ' as with conscience, both must have roots in personality. Personality is a more comprehensive term than character. ' Character ' suggests a certain attitude of moral suspicion or prejudice in the reader which may be utterly unfounded, and creates an uncongenial atmosphere in which to listen to any man who is carrying out his vocation. Personality implies contact and imaginative sympathy with one's fellow-men, and an influence not only exerted upon but received from them. What the poet ' likes ' to do with his art is bound up with certain moral qualities in himself, which enable him to take a properly exalted and proportionate view of human nature. A poet's personality must also contain a sense of responsibility for and to the society of which he is a member. The works of the poetic imagination, in Shelley's noble words, copied into the imaginations of men, become ' as generals to the bewildered army of their thoughts.' A true poet will always assume that his words are words of life, living forms which enshrine seminal ideas. The poet cannot usurp the place of the saint, the statesman, or the social reformer, although they, too, need his aid. The poet, as Dr. Johnson once said, must consider himself as presiding over the thoughts and manners of future generations. The poet's personality determines his rendering of a subject, and a reader's personality goes to form his judgment upon that rendering.

I do not mean, of course, that the knowledge of a poet's frailties should prejudice the reader in his attitude towards his poetry. Frailties would be meaningless, would not appeal to us as strange unless there were a background of sterling worth of character in the poet—as in all of us— against which they were displayed. All that is of sterling worth in poetry, as Ruskin has insisted, has come of a sterling worth in the soul that wrote it. Poetry and personality are inseparable. A poet's frailties ' are part of a personality altogether larger than ours, and as far beyond our judgment in its darkness as beyond our following in its light.' [12]

Nay, even poets, they whose frail hands catch
The shadow of vanishing beauty, may not match
This leafy ecstasy.   Sweet words may cull
Such magical beauty as time may not destroy ;
But we, alas, are not more beautiful :
We cannot flower in beauty as in joy.
We sing, our musèd words are sped, and then
Poets are only men
Who age, and toil, and sicken. . . . This maim'd tree
May stand in leaf when I have ceased to be.[13]

The actual subject of a poem is no indication of the worth of a poet's personality. The subject is presented to him, and his imagination encounters it.   It is an opportunity for the creative influence of his personality, and it is ultimately that personality with which we hold communion in the poem, and which either revolts or allures us.   Benedick in *Much Ado About Nothing* [14] says to Balthasar as he hears him play his guitar :—

> Is it not strange that sheep's guts
> Should hale souls out of men's bodies ?

Out of that unseemly material the musician has, it may be, brought a harmony that would

> Create a soul under the ribs of death.

He has communicated to others his personality. What is repulsive in the two illustrations I gathered from the gospels, the Pharisee and the Elder Brother, is not only their rendering of an ugly subject, but their respective personalities that shine through them. So it is in bad poetry. I take the liberty of quoting these incisive and impressive words from Sir Henry Newbolt :—

It is possible, then, for art to be bad art : is it not possible for it to be bad morals, to be dangerous to the community ? I do not doubt that it is : there may be danger of the worst, and when it exists it will be a much more insidious danger than that commonly apprehended. Information does not corrupt, nor does argument : if they did, science would be the most dangerous of all influences, and there have been times and places in which it was so considered. What corrupts or may corrupt is contact with a corrupt personality. Now contact with a personality is precisely what Art gives. The Poet, the artist, takes you into his new world. What you see or hear there may be painful or pleasant, but it cannot in itself be harmful : it is merely a kind of spiritual experience. But the atmosphere of that world, the quality of the imagination you breathe there, the unseen but all-pervading presence of the creative spirit, that is a vital matter.[15]

The supreme test may thus be applied to all poetry—Is it creative or is it destructive ? Ruskin has said that instead of the words ' good ' and ' wicked ' used of men, you may almost substitute the words ' makers ' and ' destroyers.' Our modern poetry is rich in the work of poets who have not belied their name as ' makers,' but a fuller understanding of what is meant by saying that the poet's aim is to give pleasure is sorely needed. There is a signal which Nature flies when life has succeeded, and out of some bit of chaos order has sprung into being by creative effort. In the great Hebrew poem of creation in Job, at the moment when creative activity begins, ' the morning stars sang together, and all the sons of God shouted for joy.' The signal is joy, a more significant and more comprehensive word than pleasure. ' Pleasure,' says Professor Bergson, ' like pain is only a contrivance for enabling the creature to preserve its life : it does not indicate the direction in which life is thrusting.' What really is meant by the poet's aim, we may venture to say, is better described as joy. Joy is the invariable sign of creation. The poetic subject may be ugly, base, or commonplace : has the poet succeeded in seeing, and enabling us to see, a secret beauty never before disclosed? If so, the accompaniment of the discovery will be joy, uttering itself in song. The joy may be grave and melancholy; it may be a fierce joy, cleansing in its pity and terror; or a joyous calm, the fruit of self-subjugation and self-control.

> His servants he, with new acquist
> Of true experience, from this great event
> With peace and consolation hath dismissed,
> And calm of mind, all passion spent.

There is also the sheer joy of living, such as is expressed in a poem like Mr. W. H. Davies's *A Great Time*; or of loving, like Miss Violet Jacob's *Tam i' the Kirk*. All these kinds of joy are a signal that an addition has been made to the energy of life. Life has been increased and not diminished, created and not destroyed.

Poetry is a real contribution to the conquest both of moral and of physical evil. Where there is song,—to apply Ruskin's words about Art,—some portion of the wilderness of life has been redeemed into garden ground. We are once more assured of the order of things, and by means of poetry that order is ever being extended throughout the whole range of human existence.

And in all I see
Of common daily usage is renewed
This primal and ecstatic mystery
Of chaos bidden into many-hued
Wonders of form, life in the void create,
And monstrous silence made articulate.[16]

The deepest service of poetry is more than that it is the imaginative record of passions, persons, or events in their appropriate magnitude. It is, in Walt Whitman's words, to give us ' good heart as a radical possession and habit.' This ' good heart ' uttering itself in song is also the test which Meredith has taught us to apply in his sonnet *The Spirit of*

Shakespeare, and in the lines from his *Reading of Earth* :—

> Is it accepted of Song ?
> Does it sound to the mind through the ear,
> Right sober, right sane ? has it disciplined feet ?
> Thou wilt find it a test severe :
> Unerring whatever the theme.
> Rings if for Reason a melody clear,
> We have bidden old Chaos retreat ;
> We have called on Creation to hear ;
> All forces that make us are one full stream.[17]

FUTURISM AND THE SPIRIT OF REVOLT

There is a generation that curseth their father, and
doth not bless their mother.

> The Book of Proverbs.

Yet, when I would command thee hence,
Thou mockest at the vain pretence,
Murmuring in mine ear a song
Once loved, alas ! forgotten long ;
And on my brow I feel a kiss
That I would rather die than miss.

> MARY E. COLERIDGE, *Memory.*

MATTHEW ARNOLD begins his essay on
The Study of Poetry with the words, applied
to the religious thought of his day :—

There is not a creed which is not shaken, not
an accredited dogma which is not shown to be
questionable, not a received tradition which does
not threaten to dissolve.

Had he lived to-day, he would have

found that his words are as applicable to literature as to dogma. In the famous essay itself, he questions with remarkable thoroughness traditional judgments on Chaucer and Burns. He may be said to have inaugurated an era of literary freedom in criticising the judgments of the past, which has not been without its effect in our own day. He strenuously set himself against blind veneration in place of study, the kind of criticism which ' puts a halo for a physiognomy, a statue where there was once a man.' To-day, all the standards of the past in literature as in religion— intellectual, moral, religious, and aesthetic —are being questioned. Personal, rather than real, preferences frequently determine the critical judgment, and poetry sometimes suffers when criticism is ruled by the coterie.

I

The movement towards literary and intellectual freedom in the poetry of to-day has its *enfants terribles*. There is, for example, a poetry of pure sentimentalism, in which the poet becomes something like an appreciative spectator of his own emotions. He elaborates his own sensations, and misses that universal appeal which can only be preserved by constant reference to nature. Some poets are like Meredith's bluebottle, which ' sings only when it is bothered ' ; others, not so harmless, also like the bluebottle, have a fondness for carrion. Every feeling of the poet, every act of introspection and self-analysis is presupposed as worthy of expression. Poetry, we need again to be reminded, is a criticism of life, an application of ideas— not moods—to life. For the basis of such criticism a real perception of life is needed.

Some perceptions are slight ; the poet is simply ' bothered,' and the sound is but the vibration of his wings. Others are coarse, not so much by reason of what is perceived as that the perception indicates a personality which dwells, say, on sex, apart from its significance as part of the whole of life. To isolate, for example, the physical aspect of sex is to succeed, perhaps, in being decorative, but in the end insidiously suggestive. Matthew Arnold, speaking of Keats and Guerin, gives an extremely noble conception of the poet's vocation when he says :—

When they speak of the world, they speak like Adam naming by Divine inspiration the creatures ; their expression corresponds with the thing's essential reality.[1]

It is just as unreal for a poet, as for a moralist, to isolate in a kind of mental complex this question of sex. To do so is also for the poet to abrogate his share in the creative function, and to misname the creature. Erotic poetry is an offence inasmuch as it is lacking in the sense of the mysterious and unsearchable purposes of Nature.

In poetry to-day, as in art, there is a ' futurist ' movement. Futurism is a revolt against the idea that the present is to be ruled by the traditional codes of the past. It makes itself felt, in one direction, in the question of metres. The old metres are regarded as too rigid for the new emotions, and the result is often a metrical anti-nomianism. A mild example is to be found in the poem *Miners* [2] by Wilfrid Owen (who is, however, no real futurist), where actual dissonance, produced by the rhyming of consonants instead of vowels, is used instead of conventional rhyme or verse without rhyme at all. In the concluding stanza of his poem, ' groaned '

' crooned ' ' ground,' ' loads ' ' lids ' ' lads '
are rhymed. On the other hand, where
you have free unrhymed verse, the object
apparently is to express in the structure
of the verse fluctuations and changes of
emotion. Free unrhymed verse may be
poetry, as Walt Whitman's verse proves,
but it is still the poetic emotion or rhythm,
not the fluctuating moods of the poet, that
is thus expressed. The climax is reached
in the work of the Futurist proper who
claims that the pace of life and the scientific
discovery of to-day have developed a new
kind of human perceptivity. The imagination of the poet is described as a ' wireless
imagination.' The words are disjointed
and there are no ' connecting wires of
syntax.' All this is really a kind of
poetic Bolshevism. It assumes that ' the
shocks and vibrations of our mutable ego,'
which this kind of poetry professes to
register, are worthy of being set forth as

having universal significance. By their
very nature, these are incapable of being
perpetuated. Art is much more than an
imitation of Nature. Pre-occupation with
' the things we live and work with ' may
easily degenerate into the purely topical.
It is claimed that the growth and variety
of modern civilisation, the speed at
which it moves and its hostility to the
quiet life, have all developed a new kind
of sensibility, which, in its turn, demands
a new kind of poetry. The growth
of modern civilisation may have added
to the occasions when we are most
deeply moved, but it cannot add new
emotions to the human heart. Our cry
has vibrated before in the silence of the
ages.[3]

> Go through the door,
> You shall find nothing that has not been before,
> Nothing so bitter it will not be once more.
> All this our sad estate was known of yore,

In old worlds red with pain,
Borne by hearts sullen and sick as ours, through
Desperate, forgotten, other winters, when
    Tears fell, and hopes, and men,
And crowns, and cities, and blood, on a trampled
        plain,
And nations, and honour, and God, and always
        rain. . . .
And honour and hope and God rose up again,
    And like trees nations grew . . .
Whatever the year brings, he brings nothing new.[4]

II

The whole movement, of which Futurism is but a symptom, must be estimated by a judgment freed from bias and prejudice aroused by the vagaries of extremists. It really arises in stark opposition to the notion that life may be harnessed to and interpreted by changeless codes and fixed systems. 'The endless and irregular movement of human things does not admit of a universal rule,' said Plato long ago. This

' endless and irregular movement of human things ' is being felt in our poetry to-day. In the Browning-Tennyson age, the conclusions of science, ethics, and religious speculation were dominant. There were indeed rebels like Henley and Swinburne, who held that ' a creed is a rod '; it is alleged much more generally to-day, that the systems, the creeds, and conventional morality are repressing not only the full stream of personal life, but in particular poetry. Life is said to be moving away from these conventions. At the heart of the movement there is essentially a feeling akin to the misgiving of Browning's sculptor, who experiences all his old standards of beauty as vain and fleeting, now that this beautiful woman, his wife, has come into his life.

> My Tydeus must be carved that 's there in clay ;
> Yet how be carved, with you about the room ?
> Shall I ever work again ?

Futurism also has its origin deep in the spirit of revolt against conventional morality. A modern novelist makes one of his characters say :—

> Conventions can be as cruel as hell. But they 're all absolutely rightly based. That 's the baffling and the maddening part of them. . . . In their application they 're often unutterably wrong, cruel, hideously cruel and unjust, but when you examine them, even at their cruellest, you can't help seeing that fundamentally they 're absolutely right and reasonable and necessary.[5]

Our age has made up its mind—thereby not alone among the ages in so doing—that you cannot enclose life in universal rules or formulae. In Tennyson's *Palace of Art* there comes to the soul a moment when

> Far off she seem'd to hear the dully sound
>> Of human footsteps fall.

That sound is more insistent and compelling in poetry to-day ; everywhere it

hears ' the travelling feet of men.'   Our
present poetic thinking is broad-based on
actual life and actual living.   Conventional
rules of conduct and of thought were
framed by a certain ' Mrs. Grundy,' who is
thus described by Mr. de la Mare :—

High-coifed, broad-browed, aged, suave yet grim,
A large flat face, eyes keenly dim,
Staring at nothing—that 's me !—and yet
With a hate one could never, no, never forget.
.   .   .   .
Why didst thou dare the thorns of the grove,
Timidest trespasser, huntress of love ?
Now thou hast peeped, and now dost know
What kind of creature is thine for foe.[6]

Conventional codes are regarded as the
natural enemy of Diana, the spirit of
mother-earth, the impersonation of the
vitality and power of Nature, the primeval
fount of all poetry.

Nevertheless Mrs. Grundy, it may be
conjectured, is a debased image of another

and nobler power that is at work in the life of man. She is a form of the impulse that creates and safeguards social life, an impulse both ' right, reasonable, and necessary.' There are two ways of building up a social code. One is by external outwardly-imposed legislation ; the other is by allowing men to legislate for themselves. Mrs. Grundy represents both the success and the failure of the latter method—of a social legislation, which, in its onward course, must inevitably take outward, and preferably unwritten forms. It has succeeded from time to time in reaching what is fundamentally right, but has failed in its application of it to concrete cases. The Sermon on the Mount makes a far wider appeal than is contained in its letter. Its principles make an unwritten appeal to the consciences of men, and also create—as all living codes must—the kind of men who have the spiritual perception, the tact, and

the will to apply it from age to age.   It
has an authority that is not superimposed
but imposes itself.   By the very provoca-
tion to thought which it gives, it recognises
men's right to legislate for themselves.
The God of the Sermon is a spirit ; the
god represented in Mrs. Grundy is that
same spirit depicted as an idol with a
multiplicity of hands and eyes, arranging
carefully and scrutinising jealously the
free movement of life.   Mrs. Grundy is
Life become afraid of its own instinct for
progress.   We may recall how the ' Laws '
in the *Crito* came and spoke with Socrates
in prison.   While his friends urged him to
escape, they pled with him to stay and
die.   ' If you die,' they said, ' you will go
away wronged, not by us the laws, but
by men who have applied them.'   Mrs.
Grundy, in her original aspect, is a goddess
of freedom, not of conventional restraint.
She represents men's ability for self-

legislation with a social aim before their eyes, and has succeeded in producing a social code which, but for her own timidity, would be continually alive and developing. The appeal is not from Mrs. Grundy the lifeless idol to a new kind of moral being who has no past, but to ' The Man that was a Multitude,' as in Mr. Noyes's poem of that name [7] ; to man as a social being, the man in all men. The extravagancies and anarchies of our modern poetry may be left to the correction of that spirit of poetry which is at work in our own day as in past generations, the spirit that inspires both poets and readers alike.

We have always to guard against that tendency to idolatry, aesthetic, moral, and religious, which besets the advance of years.[8]

> One's feelings lose poetic flow
> Soon after twenty-seven or so ;
> Professionising modern men
> Thenceforth admire what pleased them then.

The heart of the poetic movement to-day is essentially true to the first principle of all expression in poetry, and in religion ; namely, that all codes and systems are ultimately symbols, significant fragments which represent the whole.   The chemist chooses H_2O to represent water, without claiming that the sparkle of a mountain spring, or the beating of the waves, or the beneficence of rain can be included in that formula.

Our time 's a time for symbols—who can with fulness
    of tongue
Utter this widening world to-day with old com-
    pleteness ?

The spirit of antagonism between the poet and the traditional moralist comes to the surface in a short poem, *In the Poppy Field*, by Mr. James Stephens.[9]   A meeting takes place between Mad Patsy, who, I suppose, is the poet himself in a mood of ecstatic appreciation of the glory of a field

of grain strewn with blazing poppies, and
the practical farmer, who says that ' the
poppy is a devil weed.' ' Mad Patsy ' has
seen an angel scattering the poppy seed.
Every morning

> He threw great handfuls far and nigh
> Of poppy seed among the corn ;
> And then, he said, the angels run
> To see the poppies in the sun.
>
> .　　.　　.　　.　　.　　.
>
> The devil has not any flower,
> But only money in his power.

' Mad Patsy ' is chosen to stand for a
seemingly witless and irresponsible defiance
of practical and utilitarian formulae as an
interpretation of life. He goes off ' chasing
a bee.'

> He ran and laughed behind a bee,
> And danced for very ecstasy.

We may compare Mr. Alfred Noyes's
The Lord of Misrule,[10] which contrasts the
natural forces of spring as a symbol of the

Easter message with its conventional and doctrinal treatment :—

All on a fresh May morning, I took my love to
    church,
To see if Parson Primrose were safely on his perch.
He scarce had won to *Thirdly*, or squire began to snore,
    When, like a sun-lit sea-wave,
    A green and crimson sea-wave,
A frolic of madcap May-folk came whooping through
    the door :

      Come up, come in with streamers !
        Come in with boughs of may !
      Come up and thump the sexton
        And carry the clerk away.
      Now skip like rams, ye mountains,
        Ye little hills, like sheep !
      Come up and wake the people
        That parson puts to sleep.

The Church is not always aware of the value of symbolic spoil won from paganism when Easter was made to synchronise with the coming of spring.

III

In several of our modern poets a deeper note is struck. Pan has two tunes which he plays upon his pipes,[11] Beauty and Terror. Mr. Ralph Hodgson, with all the mystic calm of his poetry, has an ear tuned to hear the crying and groaning of creation's pain. The well-known little poem, *The Bells of Heaven*, is a plea that conventional religion must take more account than it often does of the problem of pain. The pathos of *The Bull* has a universal appeal. He speaks of the indignity of the caged tiger, the use of larks for food, the tragedy of the wild bull, turning away

> From his visionary herds
> And his splendid yesterday,
> Turns to meet the loathly birds
> Flocking round him from the skies,
> Waiting for the flesh that dies.

The pathos and tragedy in these poems arise from that helplessness in the face of pain which makes a peculiar impression on our hearts when seen in the life of animals. Mr. Stephens has produced the same effect in *The Snare*. In Mr. John Freeman's *The Pigeons*,[12] which describes the life of suffering children, the appeal is at its utmost. The breathless adventures and ultimate escape of the fox in Mr. Masefield's *Reynard* strikes a different note, although the escape is only secured by the vicarious fate of another animal. I strongly suspect that Reynard is more than a fox, and is meant to suggest, as it does suggest powerfully, the soul's escape into freedom from its hunters. Mr. J. C. Squire has nobly voiced the simplest suffering of the human heart in *To a Bull-Dog*. In this poem, we are made to feel that there are ranges of painful experience into which reason compels us, which are unshared by animals. We know ' what a dog doesn't know ' ; to him all beyond the senses is an utter mystery, because utterly unconsidered.

For he 's suffered a thing that dogs couldn't dream of,
And he won't be coming here any more.

Social sympathy and social suffering are frequent themes in poetry to-day. The modern poet is no mere propagandist, but he has fixed on this aspect of our common life as of supreme interest and meaning. He sees in it the significance of a whole universe. Tennyson fixed upon his ' flower in the crannied wall ' :—

If I could understand
What you are, root and all, and all in all,
I should know what God and man is.

In the social suffering depicted in Mr. W. W. Gibson's *Daily Bread*, as in Wilfrid Owen's *Miners*, we have the problem reduced to the actual concrete instance. Like the flower in the crannied wall, if we could understand what it is, root and all, and all in all, we should know what God and man is. The poet knows to-day that the unseen toilers are those without whom even poets could not write. Our life is built on ' dark foundations.' The general tendency in modern poetry is not to make these ' dark foundations ' occasions for unbelief and atheism, but rather starting-points for courageous effort on the part of those who will not ' cease from *mental* fight ' till Jerusalem is rebuilded. The significance of Blake's interpretation of Milton's genius is not lost upon the modern poet. He knows well that it is lack of imagination which is mainly responsible for nine-tenths of ' man's ingratitude to man.' The poetry of to-day which has as its theme our increasing social con-sciousness is no mere display of collective feeling. ' It is the speech of soul to soul,' [13] which, far before legislation, must always be the starting-point for the bettering of social conditions.

> And God saith, *If ye hear it,*
> This weeping of the spirit
> For the world which ye inherit,
>   Do I not hear it too ?
> Arise and to your stations,
> Ye lighted living nations !
> These be my dark foundations—
>   To raise them is for you.[14]

Contemporary poetry, then, clearly recognises with Shelley that ' the imagination is the great instrument for moral good.' The poet must not preach, but this is not the same thing as to say that the poet is not concerned with morality, and with the attempt to benefit men morally. It is precisely here that many of our present-day minor poets, in their revolt against pre-established codes and prejudices, go wrong.   It is the poet's business, in one aspect of it, not to convey moral instruction or to communicate doctrines in the form of didactic poetry, but, as Shelley says, ' to familiarise the minds of his readers with beautiful idealisms of moral excellence.'   His business is to keep alive the ' imagination ' in morality, as in every other activity of the human spirit. This is the only way to prevent Mrs. Grundy from becoming Mrs. Grundy ; for Mrs. Grundy is just eternal moral principle applied, without imagination, to the life of men.

A good example of this vivifying of the moral imagination will be found in Mr. W. H. Davies's *The Child and the Mariner*.[15]   The Mariner is a rover, drunken and a sponger, who lounges on shore as long as money lasts.   He told to the children wonderful tales of men and countries he had visited, showed his tattoo marks and told his adventures.

> Nor did those people listen with more awe
> To Lazarus—whom they had seen stone dead—
> Than did we urchins to that seaman's voice.

As he tells his stories we are made to perceive that the children's imagination has reached a view-point, for such a character, inaccessible to the ordinary moralist.

> Oh, it was sweet
> To hear that seaman tell such wondrous tales :
> How deep the sea in parts, that drownèd men
> Must go a long way to their graves and sink
> Day after day, and wander with the tides.
> He spake of his own deeds ; of how he sailed
> One summer's night along the Bosphorus,
> And he—who knew no music like the wash
> Of waves against a ship, or wind in shrouds—
> Heard then the music on that woody shore
> Of nightingales, and feared to leave the deck,
> He thought 'twas sailing into Paradise.
> To hear these stories all we urchins placed
> Our pennies in that seaman's ready hand ;

Until one morn he signed for a long cruise,
And sailed away—we never saw him more.
Could such a man sink in the sea unknown ?
Nay, he had found a land with something rich,
That kept his eyes turned inland for his life.
' A damn bad sailor and a landshark too,
No good in port or out '—my granddad said.

There are questions raised by human experience which cannot be solved by moral considerations alone. They belong to a region ' beyond good and evil.' Life must be emancipated from the tyranny of stereotyped morality. Human estimates of truth and duty like human estimates of intellectual truth (or dogmas) are not to be canonised, as though there were no prospect of deepening and enlarging them. The temptation is to live at the direction of a timorous society or a fixed tradition in morals. Our principles may be eternally right, our applications most cruelly wrong. The highest commandment is love, and

poetry is ' love talking musically.' Here
is best seen the region in which the alliance
between poetry and religion must be
sought. It is a region where their respective circles more than touch. They do
most deeply intersect.

WAR IN MODERN POETRY

> Who, doomed to go in company with Pain,
> And Fear, and Bloodshed, miserable train !
> Turns his necessity to glorious gain ;
> In face of these doth exercise a power
> Which is our human nature's highest dower.
>
> WILLIAM WORDSWORTH,
> *Character of the Happy Warrior.*

> Little live, great pass.
> Jesus Christ and Barabbas
> Were found the same day,
> This died, that went his way.
>
> C. H. SORLEY,
> *All the Hills and Vales Along.*

NEVER before, in the history of the world, has war borne so heavily on the heart of humanity as on the heart of the generation that has just emerged from the European conflict. Never before has war been so sensitively recorded in human feeling. The burden is not only a burden of sorrow, a shrinking from the appalling desolation and holocaust of life. The new burden is above all a burden of vision for the future, which, like all prophetic burdens, is also a piercing discipline. Men passed speedily from the discussion of immediate causes, easily discerned, and the rightful conviction that war was inevitable, to a vivid apprehension of the facts. Many causes contributed thereto, but a chief one was that the poet himself turned soldier. His imagination was directed on the facts as he experienced them, not from afar, but in all their actual squalor, ugliness, and filth. For the poet the glory of war has passed, and instead he sings the glory of men who could thus endure and conquer. In another and more realistic sense than Wordsworth intended,

Love had he found in huts where poor men lie.

The courage in war of which the poet sings

to-day is not only the courage which meets a foe, but the bravery of imagination that faced these brute facts and came through, bearing as spoil a loftier sense of the worth of human nature. The poet has seen the naked souls of men :—

> In him the savage virtue of the Race,
> Revenge, and all ferocious thoughts were dead :
> Nor did he change ; but kept in lofty place
> The wisdom which adversity had bred.[1]

Unsuspected spiritual powers have been awakened in humanity—powers of endurance, of moral repulsion, and of deep heart-questioning. The conviction has also come to birth that there are still legions of spiritual powers in the universe, in league with man's hatred of the new horror, uninvolved and as yet unbesought.

> O Royal night, under your stars that keep
>   Their golden troops in charted motion set,
> The living legions are renewed in sleep
>   For bloodier battle yet.

O Royal death, under your boundless sky
   Where unrecorded constellations throng,
Dispassionate those other legions lie,
   Invulnerably strong.[2]

' Dispassionate '—for in the modern war-poetry there is a very remarkable absence of the temper of sheer emotional protest. Thinking, imaginative thinking, is required, and the facts are left to speak for themselves.   The most fervent appeal is to the brain and not to the heart, to the reason and not to the emotions ; for the brain can be kindled by the imagination as well as the heart.   Poets like Mr. Siegfried Sassoon and Mr. Robert Nichols have allowed us no disillusionment as to the nature of war.   They have left us also no doubt regarding the supremacy of human nature as it towers over the brute and naked facts, and afford a clear perception that the soul of man is greater than anything his mind and body have been called upon to endure.

The soldier has begun to ' reason why,' a process traditionally disastrous in war :—

> I have thought
> Often, upon those nights when I have gone
> Fatally through the Grecian tents, how well
> Might he whose life I stole and I have thriven
> Together conspiring this or that of good
> For all men, and I have sickened, and gone on
> To strike again as Troy has bidden me,
> For an oath is a queer weevil in the brain.[3]

You will find neither pacifist emotional appeal nor passionate glorifying of war in contemporary war-poetry. You will find, instead, this constant appeal to thought and imagination, the constant desire that eyes may be opened. War is the result of groping in the dark. The blind not only lead, but fight the blind. One of the most far-seeing and most courageous utterances was made by C. H. Sorley, who combined so passionate a love and loyalty to his country with a deep hatred of war. ' We

are fighting,' he said, ' not a bully but a
bigot.' The bigot is one in whose judgment
efficiency and tolerance are incompatible.
In the lines *To Germany* he says :—

You are blind like us. Your hurt no man designed,
And no man claimed the conquest of your land.
But gropers both through fields of thought confined
We stumble and we do not understand.
You only saw your future bigly planned,
And we, the tapering paths of our own mind.
And in each other's dearest ways we stand,
And hiss and hate. And the blind fight the blind.[4]

The glory has been transferred from
war to the men who waged it. A new and
significant care for the individual life has
emerged. Even a straw shows the direction of the wind, and in Mr. Hardy's *Dynasts*
a small thing is noticeable. In one or two
of the footnotes, amid all the irresistible
passage of destiny, he has gone out of his
way to mention the names of some actual
Wessex soldiers whose names he had

unearthed and who were engaged in the Napoleonic conflict. He feels that they must not be forgotten, and we are reminded of his earlier *Souls of the Slain.* Similarly, in the bulk of the war-poetry, war is no longer ' a great community of task,' leaving no room for human sympathy and comradeship.

> Men I love about me,
> Over me the sun.

Each individual life has a new significance, and each soldier has a heart and a soul of his own.

> Here there are the great things, life and death and
>   danger,
> All I ever dreamed of in the days that used to be,
> Comrades and good fellowship, the soul of an army,
> But, oh, it is the little things that take the heart of me.
>
> For all we know of old, for little things and lovely,
> We bow us to a greater life beyond our hope or fear,
> To bear its heavy burdens, endure its toils unheeding,
> Because of all the little things so distant and so dear.[5]

The deepened value which religious faith gives to the individual life is invoked in Mr. Robert Nichol's *Battery Moving up to a New Position*, where the sound of the bell tolling for the celebration of Mass as the battery passes, elicits the longing that the soldiers' coming sacrifice may not be forgotten by the assembled worshippers :—

> Turn hearts to us as we go by,
> Salute those about to die,
> Plead for them, the deep bell toll :
> Their sacrifice must soon be whole.

Fine expression has also been given to the impulse that rallied men to the flag, as in Mr. Hardy's *Men who March Away*—

> In our heart of hearts believing
> Victory crowns the just.

A still deeper note is struck by C. H. Sorley, in whose *All the Hills and Vales Along* that self-consciousness of the poet, consecrating himself to sacrifice—which with a shrewd judgment he chided in

Rupert Brooke—is entirely absent. Death not victory is the goal towards which they march in a selfless outburst of song.

> Earth that never doubts nor fears,
> Earth that knows of death, not tears,
> Earth that bore with joyful ease
> Hemlock for Socrates,
> Earth that blossomed and was glad
> 'Neath the Cross that Christ had,
> Shall rejoice and blossom too
> When the bullet reaches you.
>> Wherefore, men marching
>> On the road to death, sing !
>> Pour your gladness on earth's head,
>> So be merry, so be dead.[6]

There is little of the noise and smoke of battle in our modern poetry of war.   It has realised the meaning of Wordsworth's lines in *The Excursion* :—

> Noise is there not enough in doleful war,
> But that the heaven-born poet must stand forth,
> And lend the echoes of his sacred shell
> To multiply and aggravate the din ?

Poems like Sir Henry Newbolt's *Vitai Lampada* belong to a bygone age of warfare. *Vitai Lampada* has gone home to the English heart, because it breathes the spirit of all that is best in public-school life. The discovery, however, was not yet made when that poem was written, as it has now been, that the common labourer, the small shopkeeper, the farm-worker, the musician, the artist, the poet, all had that soul of honour, achieved somewhere in the great school of living, which brought him away from his chosen task into a life he could not but loathe. The knightly spirit was already in all of these, ere ever they reached the battlefield on which their lance was broken.

> His lance is broken ; but he lies content
> With that high hour, in which he lived and died.
> And falling thus, he wants no recompense,
> Who found his battle in the last resort ;
> Nor needs he any hearse to bear him hence
> Who goes to join the men of Agincourt.[7]

Poetry also has found expression for a new horror that has been added to war, the horror of ' organised boredom.' [8]   One cultured soldier described war as ' months of boredom punctuated by terror.'   It is no disparagement to say that there were countless men in the embattled hosts, drawn by an invincible sense of honour and love of country, whose heart never was, or had ceased to be, in the work in which they were engaged.[9] Their heroism was that they were there at all.   Every chance of spiritual escape from the battlefield they took with eagerness, and some of the most signal acts of bravery were accomplished in the souls of those who expressed themselves in poetry, if not always with complete success, on active service or in hospital. Those moments of spiritual escape are the themes of some of the noblest modern war-verse, and in the escape we also are set free.   It takes the form of thoughts of the familiar countryside, the old home, the wonder of the stars, the sense of the supreme significance of human affections.

A new kind of love-lyric has also arisen, the lyric of comradeship, of the love of man for man. This sense of comradeship and of the mutual love of officer and men is conspicuous.

> Was there love once ?   I have forgotten her.
> Was there grief once ?   grief yet is mine.
> Other loves I have, men rough, but men who stir
> More grief, more joy, than love of thee and thine.
>
> Faces cheerful, full of whimsical mirth,
> Lined by the wind, burned by the sun ;
> Bodies enraptured by the abounding earth,
> As whose children we are brethren :   one.
>
> .   .   .   .
>
> Was there love once ?   I have forgotten her.
> Was there grief once ?   grief yet is mine.
> O loved, living, dying, heroic soldier,
> All, all, my joy, my grief, my love, are thine ! [10]

There are two crowning examples in modern poetry of the manner in which the poet has felt that his business is to reach the fundamental meaning of these tremendous and bewildering days. Mr. Masefield has in his *August 1914* gone to the heart of that love of hearth, and home, and landscape, and that experience of a life that lies all in spending itself for their very sake.

> These homes, this valley spread below me here,
> The rooks, the tilted stacks, the beasts in pen,
> Have been the heartfelt things, past-speaking dear
> To unknown generations of dead men.

War means, interpreted in these terms :—

> The harvest not yet won, the empty bin,
> The friendly horses taken from the stalls,
> The fallow on the hill not yet brought in,
> The cracks unplastered in the leaking walls.

In Mr. Thomas Hardy's *In Time of the Breaking of Nations*, with the consummate artist's few strokes of the brush, the toil and the human love of the familiar countryside are pictured as the only lasting things.   In their presence, as one critic has said, ' the Great War is an irrelevance.'

> Yonder a maid and her wight
>   Come whispering by :
> War's annals will cloud into night
>   Ere their story die.

The undying meaning of the sacrament of Nature, perpetually renewed and bringing comfort to the heart that receives it, is presented in *The Philosopher's Oration* (from *A Faun's Holiday*) by Mr. Robert Nichols.

> Though the wind roars, and Victory,
> A virgin fierce, on vans of gold
> Stoops through the cloud's white smother rolled
> Over the armies' shock and flow
> Across the broad green hills below,
> Yet hovers and will not circle down
> To cast t'ward one the leafy crown ;
> .   .   .   .   .   .
> Earth yet keeps her undersong
> Of comfort and of ultimate peace,
> That whoso seeks shall never cease

To hear at dawn or noon or night.
Joys hath she, too, joys thin and bright,
Too thin, too bright, for those to hear
Who listen with an eager ear,
Or course about and seek to spy,
Within an hour, eternity.
First must the spirit cast aside
This world's and next his own poor pride
And learn the universe to scan
More as a flower, less as a man.
Then shall he hear the lonely dead
Sing and the stars sing overhead.[11]

A very gallant soldier, the Hon. Julian Grenfell, who fell fighting on the western front, has given most observant and arresting expression to the inarticulate, so-called ' fatalism ' of the fighting man. In *Into Battle* Grenfell has gained a victory over death by his keen and vivid sense of fellowship with Nature and with all God's creatures. The puny individual soldier is consciously linked up with the great cosmic forces and movements, and even in war the warmth of the sun, the life of ' the glowing earth ' have gifts for him. The ' light-foot winds ' speed him to activity, and with the trees he puts on a ' newer birth.' There is a remarkable verse in which he describes the sentinel as holding high companion-ship with the stars, alongside which Mr. E. B. Osborn sets as a stirring and impressive comment the following words of Alan Seeger, another war-poet, an American, who died fighting in the Foreign Legion :—

The sentinel has ample time for reflection. Alone under the stars, war in its cosmic rather than its moral aspect reveals itself to him. . . . He thrills with the sense of filling an appointed, necessary place in the conflict of hosts, and facing the enemy's crest, above which the Great Bear wheels upward to the zenith, he feels, with a sublimity of enthusiasm that he has never before known, a kind of companion-ship with the stars.[12]

Whatever else is grimy and sordid, the senses are, to adapt Stevenson's phrase,' as though they had been washed in clear, cold water.' The primeval instincts of sight and hearing are quickened to a new sensitiveness, until they vie with those of God's wild creatures.

> The kestrel hovering by day,
>   And the little owls that call by night,
> Bid him be swift and keen as they
>   As keen of ear, as swift of sight.

The patient eyes of the horses seem to speak of 'courageous hearts' in the 'dreary doubtful, waiting hours' before the attack. The sense of 'fatalism,' with which alone such work can be done, receives noble expression in the lines,

> Through joy and blindness he shall know,
>   Not caring much to know, that still
> Nor lead nor steel shall reach him, so
>   That it be not the Destined Will.

Literary criticism cannot but deal, in a peculiar tenderness and generosity of spirit, with the poetry written amid the din and horror of war. Fortunately it does not come within our scope to apportion such poetry in its order of technical merit. One thing is certain. Apart from the particular merits or demerits of the form with which our abundant war-poetry is clothed, war can never again be the same; for the creative hand of the poet has out of this ugly material made another 'addition to reality.' We have a new conception of war. Poetry has given its finer breath and spirit to a shapeless mass of hateful knowledge, and has preserved for ever a deep new desire for a world whose wars shall be of a nobler and more spiritual type, demanding not less self-effacement nor less courage. The lesson has been learned at infinite cost, and we are not unmindful. Mr. Laurence Binyon has perpetuated that memory in his *For the Fallen* :—

But where our desires are and our hopes profound
  Felt as a well-spring that is hidden from sight,
To the innermost heart of their own land they are
    known
  As the stars are known to the Night.

DEATH AND IMMORTALITY

And, born aboard, my rover stark,
Dread you to die aboard ?
To lay you down beside your love
With the sunset on your sword ?
        HERBERT TRENCH, *Apollo and the Seaman.*

A Power from the Unknown God,
    A Promethean Conqueror, came ;
Like a triumphal path he trod
    The thorns of death and shame.
        A mortal shape to him
        Was like the vapour dim
Which the orient planet animates with light.
                    P. B. SHELLEY, *Hellas.*

VERGIL has a famous passage describing
the shades of the dead gathering on the
banks of Acheron, and waiting for their
passage across to the Elysian fields :—

Hither there hastens a surging crowd, to

the banks of the river; matrons and men, the shades of great-hearted heroes whose life's work is done, lads and maidens, youths whose parents had seen them stretched on the funeral pile. Numerous were they as withered leaves falling in the woods at the first autumnal touch of frost; as birds that gather inland from the deep, when winter, urging them to summer skies, drives them across the sea. There they stand each one praying that he may be the first to cross the stream, and forth they stretch their hands in eager longing for the further shore.[1]

Ripae ulterioris amore, ' in eager longing for the further shore.' The desire is strangely absent from the hearts of men to-day. There is no parallel in modern poetry to Tennyson's *In Memoriam,* or Browning's *Rabbi Ben Ezra* and *Prospice.* There is an absence, almost complete, of the conviction that even for this present life a faith in personal immortality holds any central significance. Personal immortality is no longer a thought which is needed to redeem the world from sheer irrationality.[2]

I am not concerned to test those conceptions of death and its issue, which underlie modern poetry, by reference to Christian doctrine on the subject. Instead, I would regard the ideas of immortality in modern poetry as significant and valuable, reflecting, as they do, precisely those difficulties and perplexities which challenge the accepted Christian doctrine in the minds of modern men, and deserve to be treated with all sympathy and respect. This absence of belief in personal survival after death is accompanied neither by a materialistic philosophy nor, in nearly every instance, by a purely pessimistic outlook on life. Plato's severe words about materialists—who are said to ' grasp rocks and oaks ' as the only realities, and ' drag everything from heaven and the unseen to earth '—that they need to be made better men before being argued with,[3] do not apply to the poetic idealism of to-day in its almost total rejection of personal immortality. The contemporary poet is overwhelmed with his spiritual intuitions of the common things of life. The whole aim of the life-energy is towards the development of what is spiritual—beauty, truth, and harmony—and there seems to be no place for the individual. Among the moderns Mr. Herbert Trench has uttered the most thorough-going rejection of personal survival, as in his *Apollo and the Seaman*. In words that owe something of their form to Shelley, he says elsewhere :—

> The world-spring wherein hides
> Formless the God that forms us, bursts its cup—
>   Is seen a Fountain—breaking like a flower
> High into light—that at its height divides ;
>   Changelessly scattering forth,—in blaze and
>   shower—

In drops of a trembling diaphaneity—
  Dreams the God—breathings momently up-buoy
To meet a myriad ways. Those dreams are we,
  Chanted from some unfathomable joy.[4]

We have seen how modern poetry stresses the value—the creative value—of the individual life. Each new mind has its own contribution to bring to the world that is in the making, and has its own room to inhabit. Neither is disbelief in personal immortality regarded as inconsistent with belief in the Divine Love. ' God,' says William James, ' has so inexhaustible a capacity for love that His call and need is for a literally endless accumulation of created lives. He can never faint or grow weary, as we should under the increasing supply. . . . His sympathy can never know satiety or glut.'[5] These words, however, though urged in defence of personal immortality, carry with them no absolute assurance that any individual life will persist for ever. Love secures that our spiritual achievements persist, but the individual life may be cast aside as having fulfilled its function, and therefore as useless.

Underlying this drift away from the thought of future existence for the individual is the conception to which we have referred in a previous chapter of a process of things, an *élan vital*, which is working itself out in creative fashion, using matter both as instrument and as material.[6]   The conscious individual then becomes simply a point at which the universal consciousness breaks through as a perpetual stream of creative energy. To affirm that personal energy is one with this universal stream is not equivalent to affirming that the individual is indestructible. This eternity of all spirit may be a presupposition without which immortality is inconceivable, but it is not the same thing as immortality. We cannot affirm immortality by any theory of the essence of the human soul ; there may be an 'unseen, unsounded, underlying Pool of Personality, of which our own lives are but momentary jets flung into the sunlight.' [7]

Nevertheless, it is open to grave doubt whether such a conception does justice to the full content of the personal experience even of the poet. It may be seriously questioned whether this notion that the work persists without the worker really exhausts all that 'Nature,' in the widest sense, has to teach us.   It is insufficient to describe the last 'secret of the whole high scheme of life' as

> not Good, nor Immortality,
> But Beauty,—once to behold the immensities
> Filled with one soul, then to make room and die.[8]

Aesthetic experience is supposed to reveal more clearly the inner meaning of things than logical thought, and it is no doubt so ; but there is an even more deeply-illuminating experience than the aesthetic —the moral experience. The two are not incompatible. Wordsworth tells us in the *Prelude* [9] that—

> To every natural form, rock, fruit, or flower,
> Even the loose stones that cover the highway,
> I gave a moral life ; I saw them feel,
> Or linked them to some feeling : the great mass
> Lay bedded in a quickening soul, and all
> That I beheld respired with inward meaning.

There are the two schools of interpretation : one which, as Matthew Arnold does, regards Wordsworth's poetic philosophy as an ' illusion,' something projected by him, at best a pathetic fallacy, into an unresponsive universe, the shadow cast upon it by a presumptuous orthodoxy ; the other which, after the manner of Sir Walter Raleigh, [10] insists that when Wordsworth gives to

Nature a 'moral' meaning, he really believes and has felt

> that every flower
> Enjoys the air it breathes,

and

> that there are Powers
> Which of themselves our minds impress ;
> That we can feed this mind of ours
> In a wise passiveness.

'Man, the moralist,' says Sir Walter Raleigh, 'is not very quick to recognise moral capacity in anything that cannot talk.' Nature is sacramental, and has some real discipline of mind and heart to convey to the man who trusts her. The artist's business, no doubt, is not to edify the world but to understand it ; yet no artist can be said to understand the nature of human personality—man himself is a part of Nature—who is insensible to the moral grandeur as well as the beauty of Nature. Justice is done to man's moral grandeur in such dramatic work as Mr. Masefield's *Good Friday* and *Philip the King*, and in Mr. Drinkwater's *Oliver Cromwell* and *Abraham Lincoln*. ' The men of moral grandeur,' says Bergson, ' particularly those whose inventive and simple heroism has opened new paths to virtue, are revealers of metaphysical truth. Although they are the culminating point of evolution, yet they are nearest the source, and they enable us to perceive the impulsion that comes from the deep.' [11]

There is a beauty also in the Divine pursuit of the human soul, which is another name for the innermost reality of religious experience. Two of our modern poets, Francis Thompson and Mr. Masefield—in *The Hound of Heaven* and in *The Everlasting Mercy*—have recognised that the sense of the beauty of Nature is intensified by the moral influence of an inward peace of soul, that Man and Nature are thus

essentially ' adapted to one another.'
Francis Thompson says in *The Hound of
Heaven* :—

I knew all the swift importings
  On the wilful face of skies ;
  I knew how the clouds arise
  Spumèd of the wild sea-snortings ;
    All that 's born or dies
  Rose and drooped with—made them shapers
Of mine own moods, or wailful or divine—
  With them joy'd and was bereaven.

  I was heavy with the even,
  When she lit her glimmering tapers
  Round the day's dead sanctities.
  I laughed in the morning's eyes.
I triumphed and I saddened with all weather;
  Heaven and I wept together,
And its sweet tears were salt with mortal mine ;
Against the red-throb of its sunset-heart
  I laid my own to beat,
  And share commingling heat ;
But not by that, by that, was eased my human
    smart.

Francis Thompson has here described the
need which every quest for outward beauty
leaves unsatisfied.   He will, rightly, not
allow that the very impulse after God
which gives rise to the quest should thus
be stifled.   Nature, as he says in a quaint
conceit, even in her revelation of beauty,
refuses out of loyalty to God to satisfy the
soul :—

> I tempted all his servitors, but to find
> My own betrayal in their constancy,
> In faith to Him, their fickleness to me.

I

In the teaching of modern poetry regarding the significance of the individual life,
the thought moves between two positions.
The first stresses the supreme importance of the individual consciousness of
the artist.   Beauty has the value of reality
only in the poet's living experience and
expression of it in the poem.   In his poem,

A Riddle,[12] Mr. de la Mare, after an exquisite
description of a ' sea-lulled lane ' in spring,
—hazel budding, the blackthorn still leaf-
less but in full flower, and the notes of
chaffinch and robin—asks the question :—

> If hither came no man at all
> Through this grey-green, sea-haunted lane,
> Would it mere blackened nought remain ?
> Strives it this beauty and life to express
> Only in human consciousness ?

The same thought is more strenuously
and vividly uttered in *The Cragsman*, by
Geoffrey Winthrop Young :—

> In these two eyes
> that search the splendour of the earth, and seek
> the sombre mysteries on plain and peak,
> all vision wakes and dies.

A truth of crucial importance is here
suggested. A poem is not the poet's
transcription of external fact. He does
not first catch sight of what is beautiful
and then express it ; in the very act of

expression, beauty is born. Beauty lives only in the poet's or his readers' experience of outward fact.

The second position towards which modern poetic thought more frequently tends is less intelligible. It is that God (or ' Nature ' or ' Earth,' whatever name is given) preserves within Himself the gains of our spiritual achievements, moral, intellectual, or artistic. The position is put most clearly by George Meredith in these lines from *The Thrush in February* :—

> Full lasting is the song, though he
> The singer passes ; lasting too,
> For souls not lent in usury,
> The rapture of the forward view.
>
> With that I bear my senses fraught
> Till what I am fast shoreward drives.
> They are the vessel of the Thought.
> The vessel splits, the Thought survives.

Our spiritual ' values '—to use the word that carries, better than the colder term

' ideal,' the warmth of heart, the activity of will, and the intellectual freedom that are contained in spiritual longing and achievement — are assimilated into the being of God, call the heir of all our hopes as we will, God, or Nature, or the Race. Meredith prefers most often to speak of ' Earth ' :—

> Into the breast that gives the rose
> Shall I with shuddering fall ?

lines in which again the attempt is made to satisfy our ' human longingness ' with aesthetic bread alone. This ' spirit ' does not ultimately need single human lives ; and ' raves not for a goal '—

> Shapes in man's likeness hewn
> Desires not.

We were simply required, for a space, to give expression and emphasis to certain features and characters of universal being. These features and characters persist, and go to the enrichment of the universe. The individual becomes, like Shelley's Adonais, a portion of the loveliness which once he made more lovely. This suggestion of the dead as living still in the sights and sounds of Nature is given in such an exquisite little poem as Mr. Robert Graves's *Not Dead.*

Is this doctrine of the extinction of the individual at death in harmony with the general idea of ' creative ' evolution ? Is the total sum of ' Life ' thereby diminished or increased ? Bergson remarks that amid all the forward movement of life, and all the value life attaches to the individual, no effort is apparent to prolong his existence indefinitely. There is no sign of an advance towards increased longevity of the individual. ' Everything is *as if* this death had been willed, or at least accepted, for the greater progress of life in general.' [13]

So speaks the philosopher, and the poet comes to his aid. Our modern poetry gives no indication that life, as manifested in Nature, appears to submit *with reluctance* to the necessity of Death. The sympathetic melancholy of Nature in Shelley's *Adonais* is but a shadow cast on it by human grief in the presence of Death. Present-day poetry is full of the splendour that in Nature greets or accompanies Death, and splendour is not the symbol of defeat. As in W. E. Henley's *Margaritae Sorori*—

> So be my passing !
> My task accomplished and the long day done,
> My wages taken, and in my heart
> Some late lark singing,
> Let me be gather'd to the quiet west,
> The sundown splendid and serene,
> Death.[14]

The death of Nature herself is accomplished in splendour. The leaves in autumn in their dying are tinged with a sacramental glory they never had in life :—

> Gold and rich barbaric red
> Freakt with pale and sapless vein.[15]

In the same poem Mr. Drinkwater speaks of ' the pomp and pageantry ' that begins with the decay of vegetation.

> Long in homely green they shone
>   Through the summer rains and sun,
> Now their humbleness is gone,
>   Now their little season run,
> Pomp and pageantry begun.

This magnificence of Nature in the presence of Death may be interpreted in two ways. It may betoken a complete absence of feeling in her heart, a stoical acquiescence which man should imitate :—

> We fall, or view our treasures fall,
> Unclouded, as beholds her flowers
> Earth, from a night of frosty wreck,
> Enrobed in morning's mounted fire,
> When lowly, with a broken neck,
> The crocus lays her cheek to mire.[16]

Or it may be interpreted as a sign of Nature's ' sublime imperviousness to doubt,' as in C. H. Sorley's magnificent *All the Hills and Vales Along,* and in the following passage from Mr. Hutchinson's recent novel, *If Winter Comes* [17] :—

October spoke to Sabre of Nature's sublime imperviousness to doubt, of her enormous certainty, old as creation, based in the sure foundations of the world . . . secret of its veiling mists ; whisper of its moisture-laden airs ; song of its swollen ditches, brooks, and runnels. It was not ' Take down. It is done.' It was ' Take down. It is beginning.'

Meredith, in his *Hymn to Colour,* has given expression to the thought that in Nature both Life and Death are clothed in the same splendour. In the glory of the dawn Night dies into Day, and Day is born of Night.

Love took my hand when hidden stood the sun
To fling his robe on shoulder-heights of snow.
Then said : There lie they, Life and Death in one.
Whichever is, the other is : but know,
It is thy craving self that thou dost see,
      Not in them seeing me.

Is this signal of beauty in Nature, enhanced even at the moment of death, an indication of a life-process that is making or that is unmaking itself ? Can it be that this beauty which, in Nature, suffuses the grim fact of death really betokens a moment in creative progress, when the vital spirit feels itself encumbered with and impatient of the restraining channel or sheath of human personality which has now ceased to serve its purposes, and must ruthlessly and inevitably gather it, as every other human achievement of beauty, truth, or goodness, into itself ?   The moment when

> It cracks at last—the glowing sheath
> The illusion, Personality—
> Absorbed and interwound with death,
> The myriads are dissolved in Thee.[18]

Even from the aesthetic point of view alone, such a reading of beauty seems unsatisfying.   If the poet's song is an indication that reality has become enriched and not impoverished by death, is he warranted in regarding this outward splendour at the moment of death as a pledge not of generation but of dissolution ? Should it not rather be as an announcement that life has succeeded, gained ground, and conquered, and that the passing of the individual soul is accepted by Nature neither with reluctance nor with indifference, and indeed with welcoming eagerness. One of the finest interpretations in modern poetry of the radiant and gracious splendour of Nature at the moment of the soul's passing hence is the lines written by the Hon. Maurice Baring, entitled *In Memoriam, A. H.,*[19] an elegy on the death of Lord Lucas, an officer of the Royal Flying Corps. He describes the sky on the last evening they spent together, a sunset that was the prelude to ' a soaring death ' beyond the flaming ramparts of the world. It is illegitimate to freeze the warm poetic imagery of a poem such as Mr. Baring's into any form of positive doctrine. It is, however, a welcome reading of Nature's symbols in a sense full of significance for the continuance of the individual life beyond the shadows. Its mood is a contrast to Meredith's *Dirge in Woods*, in which the wind in the pines causes them to drop their cones silently on the mossy floor of the forest, a symbol of the irresistible passage of life that sheds indifferently as it goes single human lives.

> Overhead, overhead
> Rushes life in a race,
> As the clouds the clouds chase ;
>   And we go,
> And we drop like the fruits of the tree,
>   Even we,
>   Even so.[20]

Meredith's poem is an echo of the ancient Homeric sigh, and displays the Hellenic directness and simplicity of thought :

' Even as are the generations of leaves
such are those likewise of men ; the leaves
that the wind scattereth to earth.'

II

Many causes may be assigned for the
decline of faith to-day in personal immortality.   There is the inevitable reaction
from the ' other-worldliness ' of religion
in past generations, and the renewed discovery of the sheer spiritual interest in
our present life, of which modern poetry
gives abundant evidence.   It may be that
the most powerful factor of all is the significant change that has taken place in
the general conception of ' eternal life.'
' Eternal ' is now regarded—and rightly—
as describing an indestructible quality
rather than an immeasurable quantity of
life.   A certain kind of life—whose features
are truth, goodness, beauty—rather than

those who seek to live it or to express it, is regarded as imperishable. The ocean expresses its movements and moods in millions of varied waves and shades of colour, but these have no claim in themselves to perpetuity :—

> Fountain of Fire whom all divide,
> We haste asunder like the spray,
> But waneless doth thy flame abide
> Whom every torch can take away.[21]

A third cause that might be assigned is the scientific conception of the intimate connection between brain and mind. Can mind function without the brain ? It may, however, be asserted with some confidence that this objection has infinitely less force than it used to have. The newer psychology has conclusively proved, as Bergson states it, that ' mind overflows the brain,' and we may assert with William James that ' the fangs of cerebralistic materialism are drawn.' Much more is contained in mind than in brain, and brain-movements cannot explain the faculty of choice. Poetry has here kept pace with the march of science back to an idealistic position.[22]

One other factor, not yet mentioned, seems pre-eminently to dominate modern thinking. This particular factor does honour to the sympathies of those on whose minds it exerts an influence, and is a compound of various motives, tenacious in their strength. Powerful motives in contemporary thought for the decline of faith in immortality are a deepening sense of the service we owe to our fellows, a quickened social conscience, and the growing zeal for the progress of the race. In the light of these, the desire for individual immortality seems selfish and ignoble. In view of the vast and spacious ends that are being served in the world's advance, it seems entirely presumptuous for the individual life to establish any claim on the universe whatsoever. There has been developed a completely self-forgetful passion. It is ours to play our part here, as men, that we may hand on our achievements to our children, and children's children, as the heritage of the past was committed to us. Our only goal is a series of progressing lives.

The essential nobility of this selflessness in the interest of Beauty, or Truth, or the Race is not to be denied. To pass for ever out of and beyond one's self is the secret of all great art and, it may be added also, of all great living. ' He that loseth his life shall save it.' Nevertheless, this heroic surrender or rather immolation of personal existence in the interests of a life in general, of a city we shall never see, implies a judgment on the ' worth ' of individual life, which marks a distinctly downward progress in our conception of the nature of life. Not only is the general worth of life diminished when we refuse to regard it as in its nature personal, but the character of the omnipotent and all-devouring Divinity whose ends we thus serve is not thereby enhanced. If it is the Race we serve, there is no assurance that even the total life of all the equally fleeting generations of men yet to be, is an end vast enough, or valuable enough, for the sacrifice of even one individual life. Our work will last, and it may be so ; but the unbearable tragedy of Death is not that it destroys the work, but that it destroys the worker, not the poem but the poet. The chief tragedy to the modern disbelief in, or sceptical attitude towards immortality is that the poem should be destroyed. This ' god ' is inferior to his worshipper, and in character is scarcely to be distinguished from the sovereign God of the ultra-Calvinist, who decreed that a certain number of elect souls should be damned for His own glory and the higher good. Or may we pass a gentler judgment and say with Euripides that ' somehow the god, if god he must be called, grows weary of consorting always with the same people '? There is a moral beauty and a spiritual magnificence in such self-surrender which disappears if and when the individual ceases to ' be ' ; at the best our individual lives appear to be but the universal mind talking in its sleep :—

> We wake and whisper awhile,
> But, the day gone by,
> Silence and sleep like fields
> Of amaranth lie.[23]

There is an individuality in every moral, aesthetic, or intellectual achievement which is of its essence, and the gift that is made is valueless without the giver. The doer, the artist, the thinker is himself incarnate

in the work, the poem or the picture, the
system. The good, the ultimate reality,
whether we regard Beauty, or Truth, or
Love as predominant in it, has to be
achieved, to be wrought out, and to be
fought out. This life-urge which employs
us appears and must be offered in our own
individual form. ' My battle is continuous
with yours, but it is not quite yours ;
yours helps me in mine, but it is not quite
the same. We are sent on diverse missions
and all of them are necessary to the
good.' [24]

So far as poetry is concerned, this indifference to the individual existence of
the poet comes perilously near to reducing
all poetry to a question of outward form.
The substance of a poem, as we have seen,
is intimately bound up with the personality
of the poet, and the greatest poetry is the
poetry that is an expression of personal
experience. Can the poet surrender faith

in his own individual existence believing that his poem is immortal, and a permanent enrichment of reality, without at the same time seriously diminishing the value of his gift ?   Milton became blind, and it is impossible to separate that experience so

> Dark, dark, irrecoverably dark

from his picture not only of Samson, but of Satan.   Milton's blindness is responsible for these features of Satan's Hell :—

> Farewell, happy fields
> Where joy for ever dwells : hail horrors, hail
> Infernal world, and thou profoundest Hell,
> Receive thy new possessor ; one who brings
> A mind not to be changed by place or time.
> The mind is its own place, and in itself
> Can make a Heaven of Hell, a Hell of Heaven.

Or take Wordsworth's poem of the *Leech-Gatherer*. Wordsworth's mood of dejection, of which he speaks in the poem, was due to his own impoverished circumstances at the time, and in the old leech-gatherer he has given us himself.

> But there may come another day to me—
> Solitude, pain of heart, distress and poverty.

Then follow the lines beginning—

> My whole life I have lived in pleasant thought,

without which the unity of the poem is broken.   Take also these lines from the poem on the *Death of James Hogg* :—

> Like clouds that rake the mountain-summits,
> Or waves that own no curbing hand,
> How fast has brother followed brother,
> From sunshine to the sunless land.

The sublime beauty of this imagery—cloud following cloud, wave following wave—is as nothing without the individual soul of Wordsworth who could so utter the deepening loneliness and passionate sorrow of the human heart.   If that sorrow is only a mere passing incident on the road to beauty's most perfect expression, then poetry would seem to be a matter of form and not of substance.   It is held apparently that the universe has a cherished place for the statue, and none for the sculptor.   Can Death be regarded as putting the finishing touches to the statue, and at the same time destroying its Creator ?   How much greater is a sculptor than his statue, a poet than his poem !

Virtue, it is held, must always be dis-interested, so disinterested as to make a man indifferent to his own individual existence.   Is this view of individual exist-ence consistent with perfect loyalty to a good cause, the cause of beauty, truth, or righteousness ?   Self-sacrifice is the free offering of oneself, the whole of oneself, for a worthy cause.   Is this ' selflessness ' of the poet that of the suicide or of the devoted servant ?   Does he diminish or increase his gift in the cause of beauty by refusing to attach permanent value or significance to his own human personality, apart from which, so far as our experience goes, beauty has no existence, and would never have come to birth. Self-sacrifice is not self-immolation, but self-expression. Self-immolation means that the courage of the faith that has sustained up to the present has failed at the last moment, and we fall with a wound in the back. Loyalty to a cause, whether beauty or politics, involves that I am an integral part of it. The larger and fuller the personality, the more perfect is the beauty to which it gives expression.

III

The power and habit of sustained thought is not characteristic of modern poetry as a whole. There are, however, two modern poets who have developed a philosophy of life, which, if it were valid, would render the doctrine of continued individual existence superfluous. These are Thomas Hardy and George Meredith.

Meredith's *A Faith on Trial* is written under the influence of the grief which followed his wife's death. All through the poem is a reasoned protest against allowing our human desire for comfort, or for revelation, to determine our faith in a future life. It is a determined stoical repression of the natural longing for reunion with a loved soul that has passed beyond the shadows. 'Heart' must give place to 'brain.' 'Earth gives only 'wisdom.'

> Not she gives the tear for the tear.

The 'wisdom' is a

> patience, mortal of peace,
> Compressing the surgent strife
> In a heart laid open, not mailed,
> To the last blank hour of the rack,
> When struck the dividing knife :
> When the hand that never had failed
> In its pressure to mine hung slack.
>   .   .   .   .   .   .

The desire for personal comfort is to
Meredith ' the cry of unfaith ' :—

> If we strain to the farther shore,
> We are catching at comfort near.
> Assurances, symbols, saws,
> Revelations in Legends, light
> To eyes rolling darkness, these
> Desired of the flesh in affright.

The human reply to Earth's relentless
teaching must be courage, the ' warrior
heart unquelled ' which is ' Earth's dearest
daughter.' To Meredith, both Life and
Death are our teachers. Death teaches
us to face facts, is ' the relentless quencher
of lies.' Death, like Siva the destroyer,
in the Hindu trinity, but clears the way for
new growth. In his *Dirge in Woods* the
fallen fir-cones lie silent and still, beneath
the life which surges on its glad way perpetually above them, and is fed by their
decay. Reason, brain and not heart, must
sit upon the throne.

Meredith, notwithstanding, is to be classed among the optimists. As in *The Spirit of Shakespeare* of whom he sings, we behold

> the honeyed corner at his lips,
> The conquering smile wherein his spirit sails.

Like him also, he smiles

> at a generation ranked
> In gloomy noddings over life.

Mr. Thomas Hardy is usually ranked among the pessimists, although he strives to repudiate the charge in the preface already quoted once or twice.[25] He mentions Heine, who observed that ' the soul has her eternal rights ; that she will not be darkened by statutes, nor lullabied by the music of bells.' An important difference between Meredith and Mr. Hardy is that the latter, in his ' full look at the Worst,' gives full scope and utterance to the human sadness of soul which such a gaze provokes.

For this we like him better. Meredith deliberately suppresses the instinct of grief, and regards as the final human triumph the conversion of a sorrowful soul into a heroic, but dispassionate 'warrior heart.' It is certainly remarkable that Mr. Hardy's method has led in later years to a growing tenderness and wistfulness. There are alterations of simple lines in new editions of his poems, outbursts of sheer lyric joy like *Timing Her*, the choruses of the Pities in *The Dynasts*, all of which are full of significance.[26] Certainly, if in the way through life our choice of guide must be cast between a pitiless courage — which as in Nietzsche ought to be the logical outcome of Meredith's position — and a courageous pity, the decision must be cast in favour of the latter.

One turns to Thomas Hardy, among the moderns, in seeking poetic expression of present-day thoughts on Death and

Immortality, with a strong sense of relief. One cannot escape the impression that Mr. Hardy himself is not really unhappy. His is a happiness like the happiness of the Greek, of which he did not speak for fear of jealous gods. The delight of Mr. Hardy in funeral, and those dirges in marriage may, after all, be but instinctive persona- tions of misery, ' the protective device,' as Sir Walter Raleigh [27] calls it, of ' a timid happiness.' However that may be, at least no violence is done by Mr. Hardy to ineradicable instincts of the soul. In his poetry, as in his prose, the human affection that seeks in immortality its brightest hope may remain unsatisfied ; it certainly does not go down to the grave

> Unwept, unhonoured, and unsung.

If human immortality is a delusion, and every man must be a hero if he is to gain even but a grim happiness in the struggle for life, we have still to define our attitude towards those countless failures among men who are neither happy nor heroic. Nietzsche has shown us the way, ruthless and logical. We must destroy all pity from our hearts. This way Mr. Hardy consistently refuses to take. The Chorus of the Pities has the last word in *The Dynasts*, and represents the passionate lovingkindness of the singer's compassionate soul flung out into the darkness :—

> Yea, Great and Good, Thee, Thee we hail,
> Who shak'st the strong, who shield'st the frail,
> Who hadst not shaped such souls as we
> If tender mercy lacked in Thee !

The claim for the perpetuation of the self, our own and other selves, has been often criticised on the ground that it leads us to forget that we are parts of a whole. It can be made to appear as a symptom of a moral breakdown, and as relegating even God to the background. Browning's

Prospice has been criticised on these very grounds.[28]　Meredith would call it 'the cry of unfaith,' which thus speaks in Browning :—

> Then a light, then thy breast,
> O thou soul of my soul !　I shall clasp thee again,
> And with God be the rest.

It may be at once conceded that any such longing for personal comfort is no sufficient foundation on which to rear a doctrine of immortality.　This is one of the grave weaknesses of modern spiritualism.　The pathos of the resort to the modern Witch of Endor is very deep and moving ; but very many of the so-called scientific results are discredited by the knowledge that the observer's heart is gravely preoccupied with the satisfaction of a personal desire and the soothing of an ever-present sorrow. Such investigators can have no real sense of the vaster significance of immortality. The faith that a loved one is alive is a corollary, and not a proof of immortality. Such a longing does not prove immortality ; it only makes immortality more desirable. Thus to attempt the proof of immortality is to stand the cone on its apex. No one knew better than Browning that such an individual basis of faith may be too slender.

Only, at heart's utmost joy and triumph, terror
Sudden turns the blood to ice : a chill wind dis-
    encharms
All the late enchantment ! What if all be error—
If the halo irised round my head were, Love, thine
    arms ? [29]

The critics of the longing for reunion, however, have forgotten that the joy of loving another is no mere sensation which we long to re-experience. Underlying such criticism is an erroneous conception of personality, and of our personal relation-ships. The tender bond that has been broken for a while was surely the whole of life, just in so far as it was not allowed to be the minister of selfish enjoyment and unsocial isolation. Love of the brethren is the token of passage from death into life. Browning might be made to reply to his own critics in the lines from *Paracelsus* :—

> 'Tis true, you utter
> This scorn while by our side and loving us ;
> 'Tis but a spot as yet : but it will break
> Into a hideous blotch if overlooked.
> How can that course be safe which from the first
> Produces carelessness to human love ?

The true expression of individuality is not found in separateness, but in our relationships with one another. Life is a kingdom of souls. Our tenderest and most valued relationships fit us to take our part in life. The note is meaningless apart from the tune. The relationship was all the more complete in so far as it went beyond itself, and gave itself in self-forgetting love to the world. No one who knows Browning can think that it was other than that for him :—

> Never may I commence my song, my due
> To God who best taught song by gift of thee,
> Except with bent head and beseeching hand.

A soul released from passion is indeed a soul that has no further claim on the universe ; for it has ceased to be a soul at all. Celsus long ago complained that the root of Christianity is its excessive valuation of the human soul, and the absurd idea that God takes interest in man. Such a valuation of our relation to another personality as so often accompanies faith in immortality, is not true because it is Christian : it is Christian because it is true, and deserves to be tested by the ordinary standard of psychological truth.

> Is this, our little lantern of man's love,
> A help to find friends wandering in the night
> In the unknown country with no star above ? [30]

There is no real bond of affection between individual lives which has enriched and perfected only them ; it has also enriched and perfected the lives of others. Personality is an enrichment, and not an encumbrance of the Life-energy. It is to social life that creative evolution leads. Personality is itself a creator of energy, and if it dies, a precious life-force has disappeared. To say that our spiritual ' values ' are ultimately assimilated by a lonely God is perilously near a form of words hiding a real world-tragedy. All the footprints, as in the old Greek fable, lead into the sick lion's den, but

> me vestigia terrent,
> Omnia te adversum spectantia, nulla retrorsum.

' The footprints terrify me. All lead towards, and none away from thee.'

The problem of personal immortality is in the end a problem of religion. With the rejection of the Christian revelation — a rejection whose validity is unsuitable for discussion here—we are forced to discover a scheme of things which is not rendered irrational by the absence of this particular belief. It may be that what has already been said may help to convince the reader that no such scheme of things has yet been conceived by the philosopher or imagined by the poet. Moreover, it is also certain that some serious violence has to be done to human instincts. If

> The man upraised on the Judean crag
>> Captains for us the war with death no more,
> His kingdom hangs as hangs the tattered flag
>> On the tomb of a great knight of yore,[31]

it becomes necessary also to dissolve and to disillusion the natural human longing, the *amor ulterioris ripae*.

> Why mourn because the ray that leads thee on
> Shines from a long annihilated star ? [32]

I conclude with a reference to a very remarkable short poem by Mrs. Fredegond

Shove, which gives unique expression, among the moderns, to faith in personal immortality. The poem is entitled *The New Ghost*.[33] The moment of burial is chosen, that moment of finality when dust is given to dust and the body, the familiar garment of the living personality, is laid away for ever. The reserve of the poem is conspicuous, and everything that might have been grotesque is wonderfully absent. A symbolic use is made of the words, ' And he, casting away his garment, rose and came to Jesus.'

And he cast it down, down, on the green grass,
Over the young crocuses, where the dew was—
He cast the garment of his flesh that was full of death,
And like a sword his spirit showed out of the cold
    sheath.

He went a pace or two, he went to meet his Lord,
And, as I said, his spirit looked like a clean sword,
And seeing him, the naked trees began shivering,
And all the birds cried out aloud as it were late
    spring.

And the Lord came on, He came down, and saw
That a soul was waiting there for Him, one without
    flaw,
And they embraced in the churchyard where the
    robins play,
And the daffodils hang down their heads, as they
    burn away.

In this little poem, unique in modern poetry, marvellous use is made of all that is symbolic and suggestive of immortality in external nature and in the human heart. The season is early spring. The trees are bare, but they shiver as though with life and the promise of leaves. The birds sing though it is early in the year and the cold has not yet departed. The kiss with which the Lord greets the ' unsheathed ghost ' is

As a hot sun, on a March day, kisses the cold ground.

The ghost kneels, and the daffodils ' as they burn away ' hang their heads as if in sympathetic worship. Here also is the *amor ulterioris ripae*, ' he went to meet his

Lord.' The longing is not without response.

> But the Lord went then, to show him the way,
> Over the young crocuses, under the green may
> That was not quite in flower yet—to a far-distant
>   land ;
> And the ghost followed, like a naked cloud holding
>   the sun's hand.

Mrs. Shove's poem is as a breath of warm
spring air, dispelling the somewhat frigid
atmosphere of heroic abnegation, which so
besets the modern poetry of Death and
Immortality. Mrs. Shove has succeeded
in giving almost perfect poetic expression
to an imperishable longing of the human
soul, which apart even from Revelation, is,
we believe, not without an answer in the
silent symbols or myriad voices of Nature.

> Have not *we* too ?—yes we have
> Answers and we know not whence ;
> Echoes from beyond the grave
> Recognised intelligence ! [34]

Notes and References

CHAPTER I

1. Robert Browning : *Luria : a Soul's Tragedy*, Act IV.

2. George Meredith : *The Lark Ascending*.

3. William Wordsworth : *The Excursion*, I. 77-80.

4. Sir Walter Raleigh : *Wordsworth*, p. 119.

5. John Drinkwater : *From a Town Window* (' Swords and Ploughshares ').

6. Compare A. C. Bradley : *Oxford Lectures on Poetry*, p. 122.

7. A. C. Bradley : *op. cit.* p. 105.

8. George Meredith : *The Woods of Westermain*.

9. George Meredith : *The Thrush in February*.

10. George Meredith : *Outer and Inner*.

11. Compare R. W. Livingstone : *The Greek Genius and its Meaning for us*, chapter i.

12. Thomas Hardy : *The Dynasts*, Part III. Act VI. Scene iii.

13. Thomas Hardy : *The Impercipient* (' Wessex Poems ').

14. George Meredith : *Foresight and Patience*.

15. Robert Lynd : *Poetry and the Modern Man*

(Introduction to ' An Anthology of Modern Verse,' by A. Methuen).

16. John Masefield : *Dauber*.

17. Walter de la Mare : *The Hour-Glass* (' The Veil and other Poems ').

18. Walter de la Mare : *In the Dock* (ib.).

CHAPTER II

1. Sir Henry Newbolt : *A New Study of English Poetry*, p. 14.

2. Compare W. B. Yeats : *The Lake Isle of Innisfree*.

3. Rupert Brooke : *Sonnet (suggested by some of the proceedings of the Society for Psychical Research)*, (' 1914 and Other Poems ').

4. Robert Browning : *The Last Ride Together*.

5. Stopford Brooke : *Browning*, p. 117.

6. George Meredith : ' Modern Love,' *Sonnet IV*.

7. William James : *Pragmatism*, p. 22.

8. Robert Browning : *Speculative* (' Asolando ').

9. George Meredith : *Diana of the Crossways*, chapter xxxvii.

10. Henri Bergson : *Mind-Energy*, p. 22.

11. A valuable criticism, brief and pointed, of William James's position, and also of Mr. H. G. Wells's idea of ' The Veiled Being ' will be found in Professor W. L. Davidson's *Recent Theistic Discussion* (pp. 162 ff.).

12. ' Chambers of Imagery ' (2nd Series).

13. John Drinkwater : ' Poems, 1908-14.'

14. John Masefield : *Sonnet IV*. (' Lollingdon Downs ') Compare *Sonnet XI*. in the same volume.

CHAPTER III

1. S. T. Coleridge : *Biographia Literaria*, chapter xiv.
2. John Drinkwater : *The Lyric*, p. 66.
3. Compare John Freeman : *The Moderns*, p. 321.
4. Ralph Hodgson : *Poems*.
5. T. E. Brown : *Collected Poems*.
6. J. W. Mackail : *Lectures on Poetry*.
7. S. T. Coleridge : *Dejection : an Ode*.
8. John Drinkwater : *The Storm* (a play, ' Pawns ').
9. John Freeman : *Music Comes* (' Stone Trees ').
10. Robert Browning : *Pippa Passes*, Part II.
11. S. T. Coleridge : *Biographia Literaria*, chapter xvi.

12. C. H. Herford : *Recent Tendencies in European Poetry* (' Recent Tendencies in European Thought '), p. 121.

13. Robert Browning : *The Ring and the Book*, I. 735 ff.

CHAPTER IV

1. Compare J. M'Dowall : *Realism*, p. 153.
2. Robert Browning : *Pippa Passes*.
3. Bernard Bosanquet : *Three Lectures on Aesthetics*, pp. 76 ff.

4. John Drinkwater : *The Loom of the Poets* (' Poems, 1908-14 ').

5. Thomas Hardy : Preface to *Late Lyrics and Earlier*.
6. Thomas Hardy : *In Tenebris*, II. (' Poems of the

Past and Present'). (Certain interesting verbal changes in the later edition of this poem may be noted.)

7. Bernard Bosanquet : *Three Lectures on Aesthetics*, p. 101.

8. Robert Burns : *Address to the Unco Guid*.

9. A. C. Bradley : *Oxford Lectures on Poetry*, pp. 194 f.

10. Robert Bridges : *Sonnet XIX*. (' Growth of Love').

11. Robert Browning : *Sordello*.

12. John Ruskin : *Lectures on Art*, § 76.

13. Francis Brett Young : *The Leaning Elm*.

14. William Shakespeare : *Much Ado about Nothing*, Act II. Scene iii. 60.

15. Sir Henry Newbolt : *A New Study of English Poetry*, p. 91.

16. Compare John Drinkwater : *The Building* (' Poems, 1908-14 ').

17. George Meredith : *The Empty Purse* (' A Reading of Earth ').

CHAPTER V

1. Matthew Arnold : *The Study of Poetry* (' Essays in Criticism ').

2. Wilfrid Owen : *Poems*.

3. Compare Sir Henry Newbolt : *A New Study of English Poetry*, pp. 240 ff.

4. Rose Macaulay : *New Year*, 1918 (' Three Days ').

5. A. S. M. Hutchinson : *If Winter Comes*, p. 113.

6. Walter de la Mare : *Mrs. Grundy* (' Motley and Other Poems ').

7. Alfred Noyes : *The Man that was a Multitude* (' A Victory Dance and Other Poems ').

8. Compare J. W. Mackail's chapter on *Poetry and Life,* in his ' Lectures on Poetry.'

9. James Stephens : *In the Poppy Field* (' The Hill of Vision ').

10. Alfred Noyes : *The Lord of Misrule* (' Collected Poems,' vol. iii.).

11. Compare R. L. Stevenson : *Pan's Pipes* (' Virginibus Puerisque ').

12. *Georgian Poetry,* 1916-17.

13. Compare Robert Lynd : *Poetry and the Modern Man* (Introduction to ' An Anthology of Modern Verse,' by A. Methuen).

14. Herbert Trench : *Chant sung in Darkness.*

15. W. H. Davies : *The Child and the Mariner* (' Songs of Joy ').

CHAPTER VI

1. William Wordsworth : *Song at the Feast of Brougham Castle.*

2. John Drinkwater : *Nocturne* (' Swords and Ploughshares ').

3. John Drinkwater : *A Play : X=O* (' Pawns ').

4. C. H. Sorley : *To Germany* (' Marlborough and Other Poems ').

5. E. A. Macintosh : *Oxford from the Trenches* (' A Highland Regiment ').

6. C. H. Sorley : *All the Hills and Vales Along* (' Marlborough and Other Poems ').

7. Herbert Asquith : *The Volunteer.*

8. E. B. Osborn : *The New Elizabethans,* p. 157.

9. Compare E. A. Macintosh : *The Volunteer* (' A Highland Regiment ').

10. Robert Nichols : *Fulfilment* (' Ardours and Endurances '). Compare E. A. Macintosh : *In Memoriam, A. D. Sutherland* (' A Highland Regiment ').

11. Robert Nichols : *A Faun's Holiday* (' Ardours and Endurances ').

12. E. B. Osborn : *The New Elizabethans,* p. 157.

CHAPTER VII

1. Vergil : *Aeneid VI.* 305 ff.

2. A. S. Pringle-Pattison : *The Idea of God,* p. 45.

3. Plato : *Sophist,* 246 A.

4. Herbert Trench : *Stanzas to Tolstoi.*

5. William James : *Human Immortality,* p. 82.

6. Compare Henri Bergson : *Mind-Energy,* p. 59.

7. Sir Henry Newbolt : *A New Study of English Poetry,* p. 67.

8. Herbert Trench : *Stanzas to Tolstoi.*

9. William Wordsworth : *Prelude,* III. 127 ff.

10. Sir Walter Raleigh : *Wordsworth,* pp. 124 ff.

11. Henri Bergson : *Mind-Energy,* p. 25.

12. Walter de la Mare : *A Riddle* (' The Veil and Other Poems ').

13. Henri Bergson : *Creative Evolution*, p. 260 n.

14. W. E. Henley : *Margaritae Sorori*.

15. John Drinkwater : *In the Woods* (' Poems, 1908-14 ').

16. George Meredith : *The Thrush in February* (' A Reading of Earth ').

17. A. S. M. Hutchinson : *If Winter Comes*, p. 131.

18. Herbert Trench : *Apollo and the Seaman*.

19. The Hon. Maurice Baring : *In Memoriam, A. H.* (' Georgian Poetry, 1916-17 ').

20. George Meredith : *Dirge in Woods* (' A Reading of Earth ').

21. Herbert Trench : *I Seek Thee in the Heart Alone*.

22. Compare John Masefield : ' Lollingdon Downs,' the *Sonnets*, especially IX.-XI.

23. Walter de la Mare : *All That's Past* (' The Listeners ').

24. Samuel M'Chord Crothers : *The Endless Life*, pp. 42 f.

25. Thomas Hardy : Preface to ' Late Lyrics and Earlier.'

26. Compare Thomas Hardy's lyric *Surview* in ' Late Lyrics and Earlier.'

27. Sir Walter Raleigh : *Wordsworth*, p. 145.

28. G. M. Trevelyan : *The Poetry and Philosophy of George Meredith*, pp. 151 ff.

29. Robert Browning : Epilogue to *Ferishta's Fancies*.

30. John   Masefield :   *Sonnet   XV.* (' Lollingdon Downs ').

31. Herbert Trench : *Stanzas to Tolstoi.*

32. Herbert Trench : *Stanzas to Tolstoi.*

33. Mrs. Fredegond Shove : *The New Ghost* (' Dreams and Journeys ').

34. William Wordsworth : *The Cuckoo Again.*

Index